SEEING WHAT I LIKE
&
LIKING WHAT I SEE

120 mind-eye color photographs by

CHARLES COLBERT

Library of Congress Cataloging-in-Publication Data

Colbert, Charles.
    Seeing what I like & liking what I see.
    p. cm.
    ISBN 0-944-85304-8
1. Visual perception. 2. Picture interpretation.
3. Photographs-Psychological aspects. I. Title.
II. Title: Seeing what I like and liking what I see.
BF241.C62   1991   91-90374
152.14—dc20   CIP

L.C. No. 91-90374
ISBN 0-944-85304-8

Graphics: Ellen Bringle
Typesetting: Martin/Greater Film Graphics
Printed in Hong Kong by Everbest Printing Company Ltd.

Released: November 15, 1991

Pendaya Publications Inc.
510 Woodvine Avenue
Metairie, Louisiana 70005
USA

TABLE OF CONTENTS

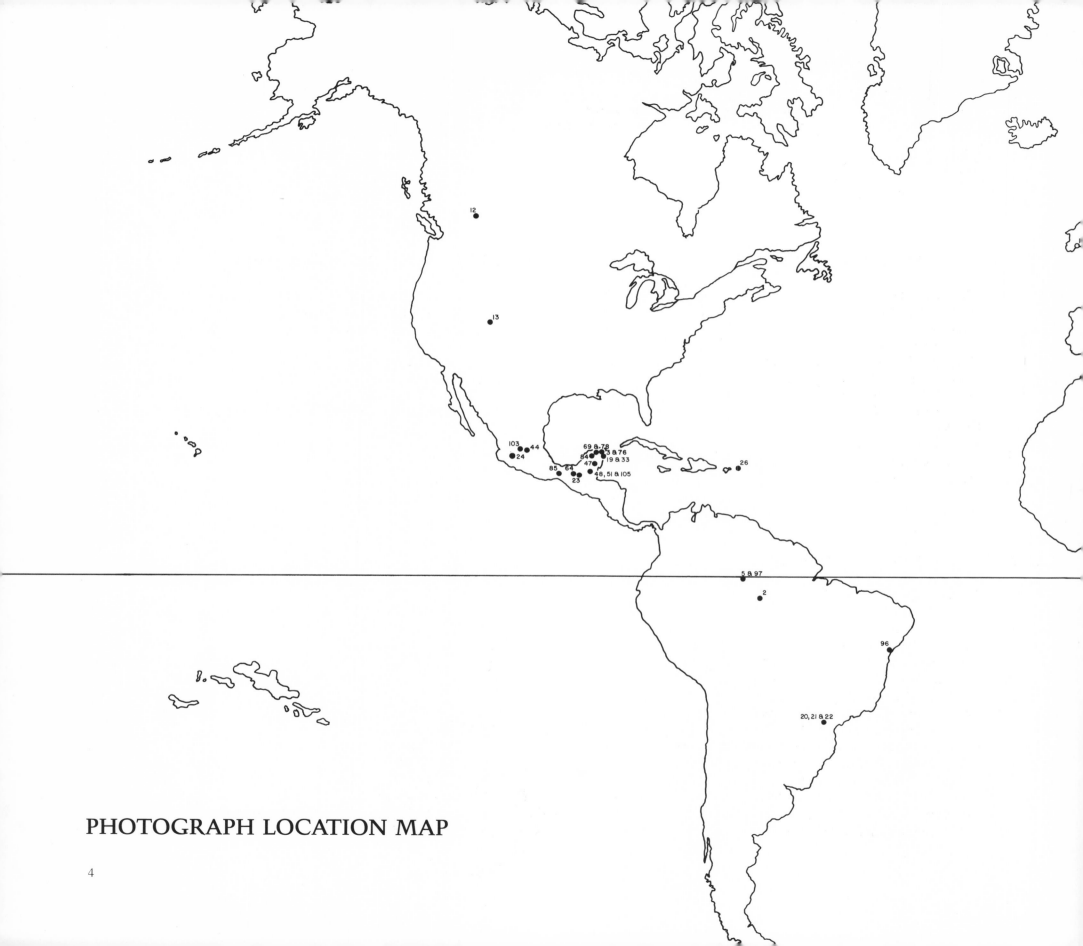

PHOTOGRAPH LOCATION MAP

4

LIST OF PHOTOGRAPHS

INTRODUCTION

The eerie silhouette of an image emerges . . . but what does it tell me? Is it simply another urban street or dreary country landscape? Seeing, I saw, but what did I see? Was it a fragment from my memory bank or mere deja vu? Why am I so unsure of the phantasm that I saw? How can I interpret these insecure feelings and assuage the urgency to understand? What portion of the image that I saw was illusion and what part is already accepted reality? A first impression seems to give existence to that which could not be and yet destroys what already exists. Is this a new insight or just another erroneous adumbration? It must be one or the other, for the act of seeing should lead us beyond what we know to what we may come to understand, from what we now see and therefore are, to what we may come to be, and then to see. Seeing, real seeing, is a primary road to learning and living.

There are many aspects to how we look and to what we see but they all produce mental images that alter future thought. The simplest words and acts are often the most difficult to understand. See, is such a word. Its meanings overflow but at its very center the word suggests a consciousness, through sight, a visual apprehension. The blind may perceive, they cannot see, but in common usage seeing has become interchangeable with understanding. "I see, said the blind man," cannot by definition, really be true. Such statements deform our acceptance of the proper relationship between mind and eye. Seeing is visual and must be understood to primarily enjoin the eye while understanding is more comprehensive and can involve seeing and a combination of other senses. Seeing certainly does not insure understanding and can be thought of as a mere mechanical function, but many essential perceptions can only occur through thoughtful looking.

How should we properly look to see to best effect? There are many ways of looking and even more facets to seeing. In most instances we must know what we seek, or want to know, if we are to look and see fully. Seeing involves much more than an accidental glance. It can serve the need to recognize, to learn, or simply to enjoy. The mental state preceding the act deeply influences the result. But, how do most of us really prepare ourselves to see more fully? How do we sensitize our brains to accept new and lasting visual experiences?

A great part of seeing, much like the act of design, requires anticipation. What we ultimately comprehend, when seeing, largely depends upon previous knowledge and half understood intuitive feelings. The preparations that we use in attempting to see can enlarge or prejudice the act. Our most significant visual perceptions are the result of chains of such accumulated insights, some planned but many accidental, as they occur throughout our lives. This path of growing comprehension and memory may explain our responses to paramnesia. It seems certain that all responses are based upon preceeding appetites.

Observation, the most critical aspect of the scientific method, apparently involves the use of predetermined systems of analysis. Yet we rarely take time to analyze what we have seen or expect to see. As our visual life passes before us, we take note of few essences and do little to crystalize our impressions. It is as if our minds were inanimate, mechanical film passing before the spot of light within a movie camera. Everything may be recorded but nothing is really seen. Because few of us take the time and care to prepare to see, we really never do see.

How can we begin to see better to interpret these fleeting flashes of visual energy? Where do we start? A common first step is obviously to realize that seeing is an intellectual rather than a simple mechanical process. We understand what we see only because our mental receptors have been prepared for a certain kind of visual experience. Intellectually we must seek causes, or at least question results as we observe visual phenomena. We must learn to abstract general rules that simplify and combine the endless components that enlarge our understanding of what we have seen. Some of this has already been done within established academic disciplines but it is important that we individually retread old paths. Such disciplines as physics, chemistry, neurology, and physiology explain some of the mechanics of seeing, while artists and philosophers have endlessly argued esthetic rules for artistic appraisal. But, each of us must develop our very own, personal weighting of values, for while we obviously cannot comprehend everything, we must bring the force of our own reason to bear upon all of our personal determinations. Giving the proper weight to visual images that continuously pass through our minds, under circumstances peculiar to our own lives, not only develops personal traits but should also let us develop a more comprehensive set of personal truths, simply because of the unique positions that our lives occupy. Our personal outlooks can involve very limited or very catholic reappraisals; however, we understand more fully if we do not attempt to comprehend everything at one time. But, where do we limit our curiosity? If we are primarily interested in the evolution of man's artistic nature should we ignore the geology of the Lascaux Cave? Because our primary concern lies in the design of buildings should we completely ignore what appear to be such irrelevancies as the formation of cumulus clouds? I think not.

It seems to me that we do not so much need to delimit our interests as to clearly define our primary purposes; to determine where we hope to make the greatest efforts to understand. By fixing the central thrust of our visual interests we will know when our forages into the unknown are either inapplicable or unproductive. At the same time, we must realize that the useful coupling of apparent nonsequiturs can create entirely new outlooks, and this comprehension is located near the heart of all creative thought. Practically, we must seek within prescribed limits, not by accommodating to socially acceptable blinkers, but with forceful predetermination. Recognizing that the very briefest visual scan, such as a two-dimensional photograph taken with an elapsed time of less than a thousandth of a second, contains information and potentially new truths that Newton, Rembrandt, and Alexander the Great could not fathom in a dozen lifetimes. Each of these world-spanning minds would see the same image quite differently. Each would bring to bear his time, state of human development, intellect, training, personal interests, and values. At the same instant, as ageless contributors to civilization, our current Rorschach test would be incomprehensible to them. Their intellectual and emotional capacities, as perceived today, would be almost useless. But, we should remember that their measure was, and is, not so much their conformity with the values of their time, as for their creative departures from the accepted norms of their day. As they once saw, we no longer see. As we now see, the future visionary will not accept. But, as we see, so we are, and we must try to see with greater timeliness and lasting clarity. The limits of our individual vision should be tested with each blink of our eyes, for infinity is all around us, time is fleeting and our reinterpreted life experiences can let us participate in changes beyond our fondest dreams.

Today, with the mesmerizing and conforming forces of the media and television so omnipotent it is seldom that anyone sees anything really new or in a different way. We are blinded by the vastness of visual images that continually pass before our eyes, whether we like and approve of them or not. Color, more intense than reality, shines from every page and screen and it is almost impossible to isolate images, or to relate them to substantial thoughts. Our visual life is comparable to the view through a dioptric scope, where multiple views of identical images swirl about the same orbiting similarities. All is beautiful, all is repetitious, and all is alike. Thoughtless replications of the same things deform our desire to understand. If everywhere we look we see the same things, how will we ever be capable of sensing new and challenging meanings?

To look properly, to see with real clarity and depth, demands that we start with a single simple object or image and seek straightforward answers to thoughtful questions. The questions that we ask within ourselves may reveal truths that we do not expect. For, as we all know, it is usually more difficult to phrase a question properly than to give an adequate answer. Such introspective searches, coupling visual perceptions and the Socratic method, may appear to rest upon collective thought, but should be highly personal and represent the pursuit of idiosyncratic values. Such seekers must deny the currently popular conspiracy of conforming beliefs and insist upon more independent understandings, for better or for worse! These idiosyncratic searches seeking an enlarged substance will not be awed, even by the threat that such thinking may derail existing social machinery. The viewer who seeks to see more must demand complete freedom to question, to wonder, and to express in new terms. These searches cannot occur within the majoritarian ethic for they demand lonely departures and a willingness to accept possible error and failure.

Since paleolithic man first scratched images on the stone walls of the Lascaux Cave other men have tried to understand why some of the things that we see are so much more memorable and beautiful than others. This is particularly true of two-dimensional visual presentations. Vicarious images, whether messages from the grave or today's ubiquitous sales photographs, include thoughts that are usually routine and repetitive but can sometimes contain unparalleled insights. How should we interpret these messages, these substitute realities? Why are we attracted to some and ignore others? How can a few of these visual communications lodge within our memory while others seem to slide away into oblivion?

Most of us are conscious of this perplexing puzzle, but artists, graphic designers, photographers, and other sensitive visualists should find the lack of answers to such a question very troubling. Why do we see and retain as we do? Why do each of us prefer some subjects, scenes, and situations and repeat them with minor variations over and over, while ignoring other opportunities? What is there within each of us that justifies these limiting acts? Do we only repeat what we like, and if so how do we know what we like, and why? Are such acts thoughtful or are they the result of subconscious and destructive bias? Are such visual preferences logically considered or do we simply accept the general values that permeate our culture? Even a thorough schooling in various academic disciplines such as the social sciences, sociology, and psychology obviously does not insure an adequate response. The physical surroundings that such carefully schooled professionals occupy and defend are just too drab and inferior! A better approach, less directed and allowing the catholicity of wider ranging thought must be found, for how often have really important creative insights been the temerarious result of a sort of informed ignorance? Why do many crude, cruel, and primitive cultures leave such sensitive and beautiful remains?

Indirect images, the photograph rather than direct vision, are all around us. At times, particularly in large cities, the indirect image, the remote, the unreal, is attributed more importance than looking directly at the scene depicted. It is this indirect image that seems to have the greatest power as a teacher. Because of these indirect images we do not need to see Mt. Kanchenjunga to know that it exists and to sense its power. We can overview the earth without being an astronaut. We can sense the operation of ventricles within the human heart without being there. These vicarious images permit an understanding that has only been possible within the last few decades. Yet this magic can be misused; an unusual photograph of a deformed animal can divert our attention from the enjoyment of nature. The created image can denigrate the real and make us oblivious to the greater substance that lies all around us; or the same image can instruct us in different new ways. The choice is our own.

Thoughts such as this occurred to me while reviewing twenty thousand colored slides taken over a period of fourteen years of travel. Many of the photographs, continents apart, were disconcertingly alike and revealed much more than the natural world that I had hoped to record. These widely dispersed and divergent photographs told a great deal about the photographer, about things that I simply did not understand. Why had I taken these views of those subjects? Was I simply recording what I understood at the time? Afterwards I often did not like the decisions that I had made. It gradually came to seem important for me to stand aside and to try to take a better look at what I had done. Through the revelations recorded in photographs taken through the years I might be able to see my actions almost as clearly as if looking at a stranger. Robert Burn's *To A Louse*, came to mind:

"O wad some Power to giftie gie us
To see oursels as ithers see us!
it wad frae many a blunder free us,"

Or would it? The proposed analysis is not intended to establish scientific or aesthetic truths. Even the quality of the photographs is not really pertinent. The plan is disagreeably self centered. I am confused about many of my actions and I want to better understand the forces underlying this series of visual decisions. Greater insight may allow me to enlarge my creative potential and perhaps even overcome the smothering social forces that make all of us so unsure of ourselves. As a teacher of building design, I am appalled at how little I really understand about why I like what I like and how I can continue to foist such uncomprehended prejudices upon my students. As an individual I know that, like most of society today, I give too much credence to transient criteria, bizarre sale spiels, and generalized statistics. Perhaps, as I attempt to explain the specifics of why I snapped a camera shutter at a particular time and view, I will be able to isolate some of the underlying reasons that make me accept such distortions and so perhaps give the reader an insight as to how I am trying to relcaim my individual rights.

As I originally viewed slide after slide it became obvious that either society or my own lazy ignorance was destroying my creative idiosyncracies. At this decisive moment two events struck me with a harsh reality. I was found to have an impending occlusion of a retinal vein and because of this I might lose the sign of one eye. The other event was equally terrifying, for having painfully stopped smoking a few years earlier, I had a powerful dream depicting my last hours on this earth. In this dream a medical specialist was telling my doctor: "Now, if he had not stopped smoking cigarettes this would never have happened!" I decided that I must try to see in my own way, while I could.

What can we believe today? Media pronouncements, seemingly founded in ethnic bias and special interests attempt to manipulate and replace traditional social mores. Communication and new truths are so instantaneous that one sobering misconception cannot be digested before another is set in its place. Scholarly journals are little better and are obviously geared to obtaining special advantages such as institutional tenure for teachers. All of us have had recent difficulties in accepting the tantalizing pronouncements of experts and special interest groups. Like most people in my field, I have not been able to escape listening to didactic young academics and sugary art historians, to a point that is barely within my tolerance of nausea itself. George Bernard Shaw's sage wit, speaking of art criticism, is even more pertinent today than when he said: "On art I am prepared to dogmatize; on traffic, ask a pleeceman,..." Today, the sure footed public pronouncements of our verbose media critics and statistical sales people are presented daily as spokesmen of unassailable truth. Pure and incontrovertible truth is always available on the six o'clock news, or carefully interspersed within ten-second sound bytes that accompany the news. Historians, limber-lipped theoreticians, and the clergy loose thoughts as though they were pellets from a shotgun. With their scatter shot they predict the future in the same way that they interpret the past, always imprecisely, always in mere patterns of possibility.

Anyone can say that they "appreciate a thing," or that they simply like it, even when they realize that they do not know why. This is understandable in the general observer, but for the artist, designer, and photographer to make so little effort to reconcile the past with future opportunities seems purblind. For the search for the numen lying within visual images, whether by selection or manipulation, is in fact the same creative force that is central to the design act. Judgments involve an introspection based upon persistent personal behavior scans.

In this proposed search to determine individual beliefs and the logic that underlies photographic decisions I want to find new associations that may challenge new perceptions. I hope to isolate and separate my deeper convictions from false beliefs; however, in this quasi self-analysis I will not limit my concerns or my pronouncements to scholarly acceptability and academic niceties. Rather, I seek the freedom of a "free fall" wherein I am not limited to any current truths or codified dogma. I can thus seek the luxury, operating somewhere between complete ignorance and pure truth, along the faultline of total possibility. Perhaps something really new will turn up.

For years I have liked many kinds of visual images and have believed that I understood why I liked them. I now find that I really do not and that I do not even understand what is meant by liking something. Like represents a set of complex meanings. As an adverb like means to conform, to compare, a similarity. Colloquially, we can know something "like a book," and then not really understand it. As a verb, like infers that an action, or condition is agreeable and gives pleasure. But here too, when used colloquially, it can mean the reverse: "I like that" can express disgust or surprise. In any event, I shall use like without irony, and with as few colloquial inferences as possible. As I use the word it means that I find something pleasing, reassuring, and promising.

It is simple enough to superficially decide what you like, know, and want to see. It is another thing to explain, particularly to yourself, why you really like, know, and want to see something. One act can be accomplished in short order, the other requires a diligent pursuit throughout a lifetime. A conscientious effort to explain our own liking to ourselves can alter our future and therefore the future of those around us. In determining what we like, in an organized way, excluding nothing but also acknowledging the particulars of our own existing beliefs, should let us look with a more intense focus and with greater creative understanding at the world around us.

Interpreting photographs, as one aspect of seeing, is much like viewing life in extreme slow motion. Each photograph represents a segment of time, place, and life. Thought of as time lapse photography the individual photograph is comparable to a single frame in cinematography. Taken through the years, individual photographs, even of different subjects, can be interpreted and constitute a dependable type of predictive activity sampling that no single photograph could possibly reveal.

The premises adopted as the title of this book will be considered in three distinct parts. In the beginning, however, the methods used in reducing twenty thousand slides to one hundred twenty photographs is briefly discussed in *Appendix A. PART I: ASPECTS OF SEEING* presents a few of the components that should underpin visual judgments and develop individual differences and supporting opinions. The components are not comprehensive but only represent some of the considerations that might be included in the reader's assay list for relating visual images and the forces that make them significant.

PART II: SEEING WHAT I LIKE categorizes and discusses the one hundred twenty photographs as a fourteen-year message from the past. Each photograph represents a single frame in a moving film; a time-motion fragment of an entire person.

PART III: LIKING WHAT I SEE attempts to explain the necessity of an animate relationship between the viewed and the viewer, to present a matrix for the comparison of rational thought and romantic feelings, and defends the absolute necessity of a personal point of view.

Beyond all of their other attributes, photographs portray accurate memories. Each represents a past time and prior event, in retrospect. Such images can never remain current but they do alter the future, for as John Locke said over three hundred years ago: "By the memory (an idea) can be made an actual perception *again*."

PART ONE: ASPECTS OF SEEING

I   THE HEREDITARY ID

We all arrive on earth much like partially programmed computers; our memory and thought processors are shaped before we arrive. The forces that made us as we are are obviously beyond our own control. We are, as we arrive, and can only hope to rearrange ourselves through our own initiatives. And, while the laws of heredity seem to say that we have evolved from common sources, we actually possess a great variety of distinct predispositions, not only in the way that we can use the capacities that we have been given but in how we interpret and weigh all perceptions that affect future change. Whether our mysterious passage from generation to generation is solely contained within our individual genes or arises from other embryonic impulses, we begin life with greatly different capacities and proclivities. From the moment of birth, our capacities for curiosity, memory, reason, and originality vary enormously. Since we do not control our so-called genetic inheritance, our only hope for growth lies in the learning that we must extract from our day-to-day activities. The innate personal traits that we inherit must be used and enlarged through the incorporation of new perceptions acquired in the course of living experiences.

The brain is in a state of continuous change. What we believe and know at age six is quite different to that at age sixty. It is in the brain that cognition, the process of knowing, confronts change. The capacity to weigh, to interpret and to reason makes change inevitable. The capacity to remember, to store, may be largely inherited, but this faculty can be enlarged through regular use. Yet pure memory is not enough. It is the way that we weigh, relate, juxtapose, store, and then recompose that separates simple recollection from creative insights. For it is not so much what we remember, but how we relate each recollection to what we thought before and our capacity to then link it properly.

How does our memory classify these continuous environmental inputs? Are they related? Do the environmental inputs occur solely from the five senses of sight, hearing, smell, taste, and touch or are these impressions so intricately interwoven with our genetic core of preunderstanding that something greater occurs? Is there a segment of our mental machinery that acts as a filter for truth, much like pain and pleasure, but is not consciously felt? Are the processes of receiving, classifying and transmitting perceptions related in ways that we do not understand? Does the judgmental and computational process, of itself, actually alter incoming and outgoing messages? It occurs to me that the very act of processing environmental observations and coordinating these wide ranging phenomena with our previous recollections and innate genetic base is a major cause for altering future understanding.

Obviously genetic and environmental forces are in a state of constant interaction. Taken together we visualize these sources of stored experience as a repository of ultimate truth. New impressions are continually sifted and tested and if proven worthy they are compared to previous beliefs before being admitted as accepted truths. The experiences of past generations are continuously balanced against new environmental challenges. Some of these functions are carried out consciously but the vast majority must be accommodated below our threshold of conscious thought.

Beyond our five known senses, where complex variables are continuously exposed to our brain computer, there must be other receptors, other points or origin and input. Organic feelings and kinesthetics that result from concomitant sense responses are also at work. In ways that we do not understand, phantasms and adumbrations of vague and delusive images often become quite real and useful. Our imagination, that indecipherable power with each of us, often seems to regroup unreasonable perceptions so as to make the irrational reasonable. Who has not seen something for the first time and said to himself: "Why didn't I see *that* before?" "That" is a new set of relations, even nonsequiturs, that have just shattered a long-held belief.

The origins of such insights must flow from previously stored information coupled with our stabilizing genetic core. But, the source of the actual observation, that allows really new interrelations, must rest upon hereditary insights that go beyond our conscious control. Whether the catalyst is an environmental perception acting upon the genetic core or the genetic core responding to a new environmental input is not really important. What is significant is that between these two forces, ideas and prophetic changes do occur.

Such emerging interaction occurring between body, mind, emotion, and genetic core must be in a state of constant flux. As life moves through its various phases, genetic and environmental dominances vary. With changes in age, health, economic need, emotional sensitivity, and psychological relations, the processes themselves are altered. The subtlety of these changes seems to affect both environmental influences and hereditary resistance and to produce unexpected contradictions. Illusion can degenerate into delusion or vague foreshadowing can grow into explicit beliefs. There are magic moments in all of our lives when things seem to come together and fleeting insights meet with understandings. As our perceptions enlarge or weaken and disappear, our judgments change. We can only hope that these seemingly accidental variables will mesh to produce moments of great fruition, for it is only then that really significant ideas emerge.

Later, as I review individual photographs and groups of related images, I will explore personal conditions and beliefs that led to the conclusive click of the camera shutter. As always, the past is prologue. Whether the rational result of previous observation and experience or the simple acknowledgement of built-in biases, such decisions rest heavily upon precedents that we can never fully explain; however, the greater our understanding of these clouded rationalizations the greater the likelihood of more productive future action.

II SYNAPTIC PERCEPTION

The relationship between our genetic inheritance and our day-to-day associations is almost incomprehensible. However, I will attempt a generalized explanation of how visual images are mechanically perceived, stored, interrelated, and reformed, as we seek new interpretations. The analogy between brain and computer does not apply here. As a machine conceived and made by man, the computer is based upon a linear and sequential program, while our brain appears to be organized within a system of random entry and chance correlation. I will outline the mechanical function of seeing, as I visualize the act occurring within my brain.

Seeing does not occur at the point of optical entry but deep within the brain itself, particularly that portion of the brain that selectively stores coded sense perceptions, differentiates light from dark, balances choices, and allows logical withdrawal of data along with the recombination of portions of earlier perceptions. While the processes used by the brain are not fully understood we do know that memory and learning are cumulative and even induce changes within themselves over a period of time. Even if neurological processes are not understood we do know that like driving an automobile the niceties of creative engineering are not essential to the pleasures of use. Before we are secure within the predictive certainties of pure science we can still enjoy myth, religion, and psychology. Ultimately our lives may reflect a kind of actuarial existence that is only explicable through mathematics, physics, chemistry, and other such predictable units of measure. Paralleling beliefs and emotions are only generalizations, transient palliatives awaiting the arrival of the only real truth, pure numerical reason. The mathematician and physical scientist, rational measurers and calculators, often question the value of loose conceptual originators; however, such romantic speculations are forerunners that lead others to prove universal truths. Intuitive insight is the conclusive final act of the romantic mind but only a new beginning for the rational scientist. Speculation and proof seldom culminate within the same person for they seem to demand very different mind-sets.

As we prepare ourselves to see, to look seriously, we must realize that the optic nerve, joining the lens of the eye to the intellect within the brain, has literally millions of communication channels or fibers that connect a small portion of the retina and a nucleus within the brain. Retinal sensors activate elements within the brain that are both chemically and electrically responsive. These impulses move almost instantaneously between the retina and a vast number of nerve cells, or neurons, within our visual cortex. These discrete, well defined cells are a part of an exquisitely complex network of fibrous axons, transporting outgoing signals in major fibers, and dendrites, receiving incoming signals in fibrous branches. Joining and transmitting mechanisms, synapses serve thousands of neurons and their electrical impulses. They also simultaneously accommodate chemical substances that transmit signals from cell to cell in layer upon layer of complexity. The nerve cells apparently communicate with one another at the synapses is an incredibly elaborate and well structured system of switching and communication.

The signals conveyed, whether dealing with thought, movement, or vision, seem to be much the same. It is the number of these impulses, within a unit of time, that apparently convey all essential messages. Beyond this rudimentary understanding, little is known about these coded messages and how their impulses interact.

It is impossible for me to imagine the intricacy of these billions of coded messages generated by our five known receptor sense organs. They simultaneously receive incoming messages and release other signals controlling our muscular and mental responses, as nerve axons terminate on gland and muscle cells. Between this receiving and sending, the judgmental aspects of reason, such as recognition, memory, calculations, emotion, and all those other attributes making us what we are, and moving in both directions, must become terribly overburdened. Is it any wonder that our response to these signals is often confused? Inside a seemingly stable and untroubled exterior, the tissues of our three-pint brain, with its incomparably complex neural circuits and countless interconnected cells, must sometimes develop paroxysms of discordancy.

When the number of synapses lying between receptors and a nerve center response muscle is small they bring about an involuntary reflex. It occurs in many parts of the body, particularly the eye. In this limited example only reception, transmission, and reaction are involved. Imagine the increasing complexity when adding such functions as a lifetime of organized memory storage, comparison, calculation, and the creative necessity for associating likes, opposites, and even nonsequiturs. What must our internal responses be like even when reacting to the calming influences of Lalo's Symphony Espanole? Why do I find this composition so soothing? Do the sounds subdue certain mental responses and allow others to relax or is the music simply a transient protective mask?

The accumulated experience, wisdom, and sensitivity within each of us can only be made known to the outside world through these complex neurological messages. Receptors and effectors are continually at work within each of us so that while we may not fully control the workings of our neurological circuits, we know that our perception can be made to grow, can become more acute, and in time can even be made to correct past errors. However we choose to explain this mystery of self-induced

change, we must acknowledge the results. The old conviction that we get what we expect and that the mind can actually alter bodily functions has a basis in fact. Intelligence and creative capacity may begin with inherited traits but they are also self induced. Few forces in our lives are as effective as *wanting* and whether this impulse will be found to have a basis in electrical and chemical components is really quite unimportant for I know that this force largely controls our capacities, our health, and our ultimate accomplishments.

In the remote future we may actually be able to calculate precisely why we like what we see, so that we could then see only what we like. But is such control desirable? What would we miss by losing our broader current horizon wherein we must search to find? Would our opportunities for real satisfaction improve or decline? Someday we may also be able to automatically give exact measure to our inclinations and preferences, but should we? Does not the process of seeking, of itself, alter our deeper and more profound perceptions? Will we ultimately be able to judge quality and the exact degree of our own creative capacities? Will we be able to understand the neurological mechanisms within our brains so that we can sit in leisurely comfort under our mechanically programmed hair-dryer-instructor, while classic Latin is joyfully impressed upon our receptive synapses. We can simply wait for this utopian nirvana of automatic understanding or we can continue to spend more time in front of television screens to achieve much the same result. We can always accept someone else's opinion as our own, or we can readapt to the insecurity of independent action and think for ourselves.

It seems to me that we should live today to the fullest, acknowledging our inherited and imposed limitations, including the potential for error in many of our efforts. Our only hope for participating in significant change is to tolerate the jangling impulses of insecure synapses, and attempt in our own independent ways to understand what is right and beautiful.

We may never be able to plot the innermost workings of our brains, and speaking as a twentieth-century savage I hope that we do not, for if this very superficial discussion has any value, it convinces me that reason, wherever its elemental electrical circuits and centers are located, demands that we must be extremely conscious of what we are individually and how important it is to properly apply our delicate sense receptors to all that is around us, in our own way.

III   CYCLES OF CHANGE

The ability to think does not begin as a summary of benign hereditary influences. It starts, as I see it, in disorder, trauma, and psychological stress. Our brain must physically enter this world in a state of great shock and distraught feelings. As we are thrust into life the sensations of cold, light, and sound must be overpowering. The naked sensitivity that we all feel as we abandon the warm and stable confines of a controlled and subordinate world must be appalling. From the blackness of another world our senses are instantly overpowered by mystifying changes. The brilliance of sound, light, and pain collapses around us as we enter an environment of eternal change and ultimate challenge. But our senses do soon come into focus and we perceive movement. Shortly afterward the joy of taste and the pain of hunger are mixed and a lifetime of smiling and crying begin.

In these early hours and weeks of life we recognize shapes and sounds and then associate them with sources and objects. We begin as pure observers with little power to act but with enormous curiosity and acuity. The capacity for memory and an ability to interpret abstract inferences is never greater. With time to lie and cogitate this strange new situation we begin to discriminate. Here, heredity and the power of prophetic new associations join and are given free range. This is a time of unsurpassed intellectual growth.

In this the first and most formative of our life cycles, what are the most powerful influences upon our newly arrived, vacant, and sponge-like brain? Emotional, mental, and physical developments race forward between sleep and fleeting moments of vital comprehension. Are our major visual impressions related to recognizing shape, color, size and contrast? When is color first really perceived? What are our most lasting and far reaching comprehensions at this time? How do these earliest influences alter our capacities in later life?

I believe that for the first few months following birth, when not hungry or in pain, that a child's consciousness is dominated by sounds, colors, and shapes and their association with objects near at hand. Here the roots of worldly understanding and appreciation begin. Sound, shape and color come into existence long before words. The senses of taste, touch, and smell must be followed by hearing and seeing. Emotional linkages occur alongside muscular development. Beyond fuzzy shapes, among shades and shadows, specific objects and colors coalesce. The blue of the sky, the green of the lawn are eagerly engraved upon our consciousnesses, while we lie on our backs, idle and apparently insensate.

As we later stand erect in our playpen, ever new perceptions and responses evolve, new muscle movements occur as clouds float by, birds sing, water reflects, trees wave, rhythm pulsates, and curious new objects attract our attention. The compounding of the senses of sight, sound, taste, smell and feel trigger an incipient imagination. The impersonal becomes touchable and produces pain or pleasure. We recognize day from night, rain and sun. The utter complexity of the most simple of life's functions is first impressed upon us. The threshold of later memories is about to occur.

Upon our release from the playpen to the enlarged world of home, yard and neighborhood objects become more manipulable. Muscular and emotional development continues and we begin to investigate the independence of our own minds and bodies. Memory becomes important in daily events. Morning, afternoon, and night are defined by the activities assigned to each. The seasons are recognized. Our toys grow in complexity and responsiveness. We differentiate and are introduced to more abstract thoughts and our drawings become more than mere scribbles. Family and human relationships, status and desirability are clarified. Romantic potentials and conceptual enlargements let us grasp "The Little Red Train That Tried" and our toy airplanes can fly so high that they touch the stars. Fantasy and miracles are real. All is possible. Fairy tales enthrall. We learn the disciplines of the alphabet and to tell time. Round is not square and toys reinforce this fact. Red is coded differently to blue. Everyone remembers their first little red wagon. We learn to count. Development races forward at an almost incomprehensible rate and the seeds of a growing judgment seem to lie in every act. We are now dry sponges lying in a succulent warm liquid.

Later, using the definitions presented by Alfred North Whitehead in *The Aims of Education*, the cycle of romantic thought is followed by the cycle of specificity, which in turn is followed by a period of generalization. The exact chronological age at which these cycles, or categorized types of response occur, varies widely and is not really pertinent to the point that I would like to make. My point is that certain perceptions, based upon growing physical skills and mental and emotional development, occur in a series of minor revelations, as we grow and mature. The recollection of these episodes, which are almost never consciously recognized at the time, seem to underlie later judgments, particularly as we respond to vicarious visual situations.

So, as we attend school and are molded to achieve an acceptable social conformity, the cycles of specificity and generalization merge. Interpersonal relations are associated with mathematics and economics. The social and the natural sciences overflow one another even though we usually correlate size, distance, and measure (specificity) before progressing into such abstractions as philosophy and world trade (generalizations). We seek individual expression, calculate, acknowledge sexual differences, race and religion. At this time religious mythologies are introduced at home with great certitude while scientific logic and reason are carried forward at school. Pride and the universal drive for recognition and power grow and personal discipline developes. We acknowledge personalized intellectual preferences and recognize the beauty of geometry, calculate rythms, and a good rejoinder. Invention is recognized and rewarded and the seductive beauty of orderly arrangements, whether flowers, numbers, muscles, or automobiles is grasped. Aesthetic principles are coupled with the observation of natural phenomena. Our powers of comprehension and order are guided, whether by instruction in biology or through the drawing of plaster casts of classic Greek sculpture. We seek to establish our mental and artistic standing and to measure ourselves alongside our peers.

Growth and change, so imperceptible within ourselves in earlier years, become apparent with a rush of endless new apprehensions. We are now conservative teenagers simply because changes are occurring so rapidly that we don't have time and power for rebellion. But, this too is growing. The scope of our comprehensions seems overpowering. We have everywhere to go, everything to understand, everything to do. At this juncture we do not realize that the seeds of these sweeping desires were undoubtedly sown years before, probably as we watched cumulus clouds float above while a diaper was changed, or as we clung to the top rail of the playpen to stand erect. The seeds of our current thoughts, or change, are always buried in the mysteries of our own past, our own earlier thoughts. What else is psychiatry about?

As puberty overtakes us, new sensations permeate our thinking. Everything assumes new values and has new possibilities. Sensuous curves and seductive shapes become more than childhood recollections. Brancusi, Arp, and Leda and the Swan are seen, and felt, in a new light. Touch joins vision in a mysterious new way. Aloneness is not the same. The allure of tenderness and an intangible response to warm colors and sentimental soft focus vision may last the remainder of a lifetime and express itself in our taste for many types of visual images. Independence, loneliness, and nostalgia are all caught up in a flurry of altered sensations.

Following adolescence these elaborate feelings expose the practical reality that life and love must be supported and paid for. Advanced study, leaving home, marriage, and children demand lasting decisions and a balance between the desirable and the possible: personal and professional moralities, hobby and business, satisfaction and profit, dream and reality. Taxes, mortgages, contracts, and all manner of social encumbrances arise to subvert the independence and the freedom that we want so much. We are forced to compromise, to settle for less than the whole, the ideal; to accept illusion for what we really believe, to adopt an avocation to save our sanity from the necessity of thinking about what we must do to simply survive. Sublimation of thought and act come to exist as daily necessities. Choices simply must be made, often quite offensive ones, and we develop an array of justifications to satisfy our conscience. We must think, discriminate, and then justify to ourselves. That is our only real option. The process of reasoning that underlies these decisions is much the same as the methods required in grading a visual image just before the camera shutter snaps. Reason and compromise are enveloped in a Laocoon convulsion of unavoidable entanglements.

It is during such a period of maturing reality that we constantly compare our opportunities with our potentials and must then develop the capacity to discriminate between the many forces that comprise our lives. Comparison and contrast become daily necessities. We are required to weigh the dissimilar and through these often unfair choices to gauge our personal relationship with life and the infinite. We love our children but often in misdirected self defense ignore our parents. We are outraged and yet accepting. During this cycle of life we dream limited dreams and accommodate our desires to those of orthodontists and college tuitions that lie ahead. We are economically fettered as lust gradually leaves us and we descend into the warm bathwater of mere acceptance. We compromise our hopes while continuing to dream of what might have been. We recognize the vicissitudes of coming age and bury ourselves in introspection. We travel, not so much to grow and to learn as to escape. We no longer seek alternatives to our vocations, but to our avocations, for opportunities to assuage the pain. As designers we may look less at buildings and more at land locations to serve dream potentials. Our views of life and everything that it consists of is again changing. But, we are still learning. We are more sure of what we like, and significantly, we don't mind admitting it in public even when it offends the status quo.

The transition is subtle but we are approaching what has been euphemistically called the "golden years." Our responsibilities have lessened along with our sense of immediacy. Aloneness is more tolerable, almost desirable. Pain is not quite so acute. We can more comfortably accept our limitations and either languidly soak in the remains of earlier religious beliefs or angrily cast them off. So, we are to die! What's to lose? At least the ashes won't be in our mouths. So what, if we enjoy a little prejudice, if it is not of a religious nature! As bigots we are not disconsolate for at least we believe in something! Now we can forsake the hypocrisy so widely accepted by society. At last we can afford to say what we believe. We have had the opportunity to observe, experience, and believe that a liberal can be obstinately opposed to what is right. We have also seen conservatives stand for constructive change.

In this mature cycle of life we can scan visual images, whether on television screens or in magazines, we can demand a personal interpretation of truth. We can reflect and build upon our own experiences to gauge the quality of the vague, the distant, and the distorted. Within our own capacity for reason, we can believe that like the elemental carbon atom, as a source of life throughout the universe, what we have seen and felt also applies to others. We can judge from, and by, what we are. The visual image is what it seems to be. It represents reason and experience that conveys a special meaning.

And yet in our mature years we may continue to seek, not truth, but identity. Who am I? Each judgment that I make tells me a bit more about who I am, and it says the same to others who can read the message. The snap of the camera shutter may reveal a landscape, but much more important it reveals another aspect of what I thought. I am always reminded of the importance of this introspection each time that I see a challenging television image. When I do I always remember that I am not the first to see and to judge the picture. The recording eye of the photographer was there before me. His thought preceded mine and my opinion is limited or enlarged by the way in which the television tube records his vision. Or, I can accept the vision as a natural event, God given, only subject to my own analytical capacities wherein my thoughts constitute the only valid explanation. The picture taker and the picture viewer can be equal partners. They should be. When they are, a miracle occurs. A fleeting moment of oneness enmeshes the seer and the thinker, the photographer and the observer. Or, as you study a photograph, should you assume that you took the picture? Do you gauge the photographer's other options and potentials? Or, are you misjudging and comparing your values against those of the unknown photographer?

Unquestionably age, sex, and state of mind affect all of our opinions. To escape clumsy preferences and inept beliefs we would all like to have a personal procedure for proper seeing. We would like for this personal method of analysis to support, and potentially expand upon, what we have already experienced. The cycles of evolving understanding sketched above should all affect future thought. Within our subconscious mental processes I believe that real insights emanate from each of these stages, or cycles, and then grow through the rest of them. The fact that is most difficult to accept implies that applied significance is random. What we think adds-up differently under many conditions. Memory traces of little red wagons, fleecy white clouds, green lawns and birds singing in spring-time can come together in vastly different ways, to enlarge, support, and to explain or to be altered by a new situation. These critically perceived environmental impressions seem to act at intersections between stored experience, heredity, and the image before us, perhaps somewhat akin to the actions of axons, dendrites, and synapses. Like random addition, very different individual amounts produce identical sums ($8+3+5+2=18$ and $15+1+1+1=18$).

As each of us traverses the cycles of life briefly described above, certain impressions are indelibly inscribed upon our conscious and subconscious minds. These perceptions, greatly influenced by inherited characteristics, alter impressions that follow as each stage of development passes before our changing point of view. The visual images of a lifetime have some unitary characteristics but each of these identifying qualities is different because the forces acting upon us are not the same and never seem to agree. These variables are the primary cause of our evolving individuality.

To again refer to Whitehead's three stages of thought we must remember that like Ballantine Ale's logo, these three circles are ever overlapping and revolving. From childhood onward we are simultaneously engrossed in all three stages of Romance, Specificity, and Generalization. It is merely the percentage, or allocation, of each of the others that varies. In relation to the cycles I visualize we are always predominantly in either Generalization, Specificity, or Romance, but we are certainly involved with the other two at all times.

As visual images pass a point of primary mental focus we assess them and put them into memory pockets largely based upon fragments of earlier determinations. Like color slides taken decades ago and just reviewed, we understand parts of these messages, as we saw them years ago, but we now summarize their significance quite differently. The house of cards that we call memory is built of shards of confused sensual perceptions. We are perpetually restructuring its overall composition and while many, even most, of our perceived truths remain intact and consistent others continue in a state of unstable change. A total equilibrium is never reached. Each visual response reminds us of past truths, now slightly altered. Over time these minor alterations within our memory bank build a new truth from our past oversights and mistakes.

As we progress from birth, through the playpen, home and neighborhood, school and puberty, leaving home and marriage and children, maturity and into the "golden years" some of our experiences and beliefs remain constant but in others there is animated change. A little red wagon has different meanings at each stage in life's cycles of change. It is considered desirable in different ways and this view alters other beliefs. The memories of singing birds in springtime, floating cumulus clouds, green grass, Brancusi's Bird, a Jaguar roadster, a pink blouse, all represent highly distinctive perceptions of sensations and experiences. Each is far greater than such minor and isolated incidents would seem to justify. Each represents a chain of responses that we assemble quite differently during the evolving stages of our life.

Such seeming casual experiences can become symbols of great substance. They tell us what we thought, at a particular time, and even more telling, what we felt. As they combine with inherited proclivities they become the building blocks of our entire future. What they really mean, regardless of any opposing intellectual explanations, is what importance we choose to assign to them. Here is the art, the conundrum of life and living, the explanations of ourselves that we make to ourselves. As we really look we must explain what we see, to ourselves. It doesn't matter who took the picture.

IV MEMORY AND SYMBOLS

The human brain gives us the capacity to return to an earlier condition. We call this memory. But what is memory? Is it merely a container in which images and perceptions are stored? Are perceptions first recognized and then stored, or must they first enter the memory and then be reorganized as they are withdrawn? No one knows. In any event, perception is much more than a matter of receiving messages from stimulated sense organs. What we see is obviously related to learning and earlier interpretations. The exchanges between perception, reason, and memory must occur so that messengers continuously move between all three.

Our memory gives us the power to recall, to reproduce what we have learned, and this must include unconscious associative mechanisms. These passively acquired experiences require the persistent modification of our behavior and mental patterns. As we seek a growing comprehension of the world, where do we place our daily findings and how do we integrate these perceptions with those that occurred years ago? Within our brain, how does our memory store such vastly diversified scenes, associations, and beliefs? How does our labile memory record and control dissimilarities and nonsequiturs and yet make them subject to instant recall, even over the span of a lifetime? How is our memory physically arranged to record and maintain its contents? In particular, how does it relate first-hand experience (neural perceptions) with vicarious generalizations (learned concepts)? How are these relations altered and reintegrated through the cycles of change discussed earlier? How does our memory make, accept, and use symbols?

As a person profoundly unlearned in such matters I will speculate upon some of these unknowns, for it seems to me that our memory and the computer have many commonalities. Among other similarities, some form of digital conversion code must serve the memories of both man and machine. Where this occurs, and how these codes can be made immediately accessible, while lastingly retained in the brain is a mystery, particularly since conditions there must always be in a state of palpitating flux. Scenes, associations and beliefs must be cross coded so that the essences of any scene, any mass perception, can have portions withdrawn, one at a time, and then instantly be weighed against a vast number of other comparable units. These impersonal and cross-coded units of memory apparently stand for many generalized things by reason of relationship, contrast, or convention. Apparently, one aspect of a thing can be expressed in terms that are understandable in many other ways. This vicarious understanding between several elements must exist since expressions occur indirectly through third party associations. Certainly our memory is not a single simple container, or even a series of file drawers, but is more likely equivalent to a world-spanning telephone system with switching exchanges at every crossroads. The entire system is contained in only a small portion of our three-pound brain. I am told that our memory is never effectively used or even fractionally filled, as we pass through the cycles of our "four score years and ten." There is always more space in our memory if we choose to use it.

Our memory then must be a vast array of multifaceted symbols that accumulate data that can be simultaneously interpreted in many ways. As we externalize these vastly complex systems of emblematic units we can develop another, but potentially related, set of metaphors and similes. Both internal and external symbolic systems have one thing in common, they represent comparisons, a realization by association, something standing in the place of something else. They substitute abstract representatives for a group of concrete objects or discrete concepts. These coded symbols can also be visible single objects standing for, or suggesting, something otherwise invisible or intangible. Sculpture and decoration often represent such applications. When cut into the lasting surface of stone, symbols often represent abstract thoughts or conditions that are much more complex than the physical objects that they depict. To the viewer's mind these symbols take on a semblance that is meant to be recognized by association with something else; such as the lion as guardian of Greek temples or as an emblem of transcendent power. Used in these multifaceted ways the symbol often represents something having an almost independent existence.

While definitions inevitably change, memory symbols, as I understand them, rest upon the physical and intellectual constructions of man. As either objects or as abstract conceptions they can only exist because of human reason. This gives them particular importance, for almost everything that we perceive has symbolic content. Most of these representations are conscious creations but many are not. Symbolic relationships that we take for granted are essential to daily life and communication. There simply must be a close correlation between our understanding of symbols and the operation of our memory. For instance, metonymic words, transposed verbal symbols, react with other word combinations to suggest new interpretations and thus allow a growing refinement of meaning to occur within our sentient memory. This enlarging comprehension seems to occur near the edge of conscious thought.

The substitution of abstract representations to take advantage of symbolic efficiency is very old. Vernacular languages and ancient artistic expressions, occurring continents and millennia apart, often have striking similarities. A comparison of ancient Egyptian, Indian and Mayan cultures proves that many of the graphic symbols that we now use developed independently of one another and under greatly different circumstances. These external similarities may be based upon the internal conformities within all men's minds. Assuming the validity of the Darwin-Wallace theory of evolution I like to think in Loren Eiseley's terms that several sea creatures, in places quite remote from one another, may have wiggled ashore at the same time for a related but distinctly different evolution.

In recent years the literary term "metaphor" has been used in aesthetic discussions to suggest a likeness or analogy between different objects or functions. In this way the word is often used almost interchangeably with symbol. But words and descriptions are not finite objects. They are symbols too, but more plastic and manipulable than objects. Their meanings change whereas objects remain the same with only their descriptions changing. The cross had distinctly different meanings for the Maya and for the Christian, but the crucifix shape is the same. The swastika may have been a symbol of good luck to earlier cultures such as in India, Persia, and the Orient but certainly not during the twentieth century in Europe. Defined as a reformed Greek Cross, assembled from four capital gammas, the swastika can be easily reshaped to become a gamma cross or gammadion. Can a swastika be reasonably interpreted to be a metaphor for a cross? Is it the physical profile, the visual shape, the verbal description or the transient interpretation that should take precedence in our thoughts and memory? Is this comparison an implicit metaphor? I believe that it is and that this is a good example of how symbols can be used and confused.

In contrast, the simile is valuable in clarifying such symbols. A simile is a figure of speech, or a visual reference, comparing two essentially unlike things. The comparison supposedly lends strength of expression, for example: "as Swastikas are reformed Greek Crosses," or as in: "like crucified on a swastika." Symbols sometimes confuse similes and vice versa. Such confusion can reasonably be assumed to occur within the digital code used by our chemically and electrically circuited memories. I believe that such irregularities must exist for their value in helping us compare and recompose the ridiculous, the inexplicable, and the multiple meaning. We learn by comparing and sometimes combining the contradictory, the absurd, and the preposterous. The value of such action lies in seeking out new perceptions, recombining non sequiturs and inverting and transposing accepted beliefs. The dissection and reassembly of accepted truths can be of great value since new visions often grow from a closer examination of premises that may have been fallacious but now represent a new potential when reassembled in a different way.

Throughout our lives, as we see, and interpret, we utilize many subjective symbols. We allow these semi-conscious representatives to act through one another to define deeper relationships for both direct and indirect comparisons. I believe that these symbols, metaphors, similes, and emblems have lives of their own. They are multiply interpretable comprehensive representations of our beliefs, at moments in time. They allow us to stand back from ourselves and to appraise our own beliefs as if seen by a stranger.

It can be logically reasoned that our entire lives are ongoing allegories. We obviously live by symbols and normative generalizations of our own making. Truth is often no more than our own applied fiction. We believe and therefore we are. Isolated acts commingle to appear as related parts of a comprehensive whole. For our mental health we develop figurative and symbolic defenses. We explain our thoughts and acts by organizing prearranged stories for ourselves. We try to simplify the incomprehensibility of life, we grope, we combine and relate acts with incoherent beliefs. We place what we learn in imaginary baskets and flag them with symbols, even before we reach the age of reason. Some of these symbols may be a part of our blastogenic core, our genetic inheritance. They are certainly conveyed to us from throughout all epochs of history and our own lives. These symbols are not always interpretable and are only important for what we believe them to mean. They can release the most complex comprehensions and adapt them for use. A traffic light, a single middle finger raised high, a dangling Tau Beta Pi key, each represent an underlying store of abstract beliefs, relate objective acts to potential consequences, and put the unstated message in visible form. All three are symbols of significance, when properly interpreted. Within a fleeting glance they compress complex explanations into milliseconds of potential comprehension.

Life can be said to rest upon such representational symbols, for it is difficult to conceive of any widely used and understood object, act, or concept that has not at some time achieved symbolic content. We depend upon these generalized summaries in almost every daily decision, so that for normal use, we do not need to fully analyze each act, each scene.

Some external and objective symbols are universal, some less accepted, and others are largely related to simple physical acts. Some of our most utilitarian symbols have evolved through time and recorded history, such as the physician's Caduceus, while others are created by each of us, individually, from living experiences. All represent a search for simplicity, clarity, and a fuller understanding. The upraised hand of peace or the grimacing death mask, such as the Balinese Rangda, are universally accepted throughout the quasi-civilized world. So it is with symbols of danger such as the yellow flag of quarantine and the skull-and-crossbones of poison or the skull of death. Functional and psychological symbols and figurative representations are also founded in natural phenomena. For instance, natural colors have long been symbolically interpreted. Blue, represents sky, water, cool, calm; red, relates to fire, blood, heat, and agitation; green, is associated with wholesome growing things; black (no color), has come to infer night, evil, mystery, hell; and white (all colors), stands for light, purity, and knowledge—but it can also symbolize death in the orient. The seasons of the year have been interpreted in much the same way throughout the ages. Spring is a happy time of rebirth, life and planting while summer is a period of growth, sunshine, joy and leisure. Autumn is associated with harvest, color and approaching old age while, winter reminds us of hibernation, lethargy and death. Within such widely accepted symbols as the seasons and colors lie layer upon layer of supporting interpretations. Pumpkins for autumn, forsythia for spring, such symbols of recognition create their own sublevels, apparently ad infinitum. Who can read Bulfinch's stories of Greek mythology and ever again be limited to a literal interpretation of life?

Such widely held symbolic images underlie most psychic and religious beliefs. Symbolic man seems to reach a zenith of uncritical acceptance, not in the mathematical symbols of esoteric science, but within veiled religious mythology and church mythomania. The fanciful early Christians, for instance, related God, Christ, and the Church to the human eye and a fish. They probably originated as graphic symbols because they were easily drawn and reproduced and were therefore effective in spreading the faith to the illiterate masses. As religious logograms they reduced abstract beliefs to understandable generalizations in much the same way that barber poles tell of barbershops or three golden balls announce hock shops. Today, corporate logos and trademarks purvey comparable symbolism, whether a Ford Motor ellipse or the acronym of International Business Machines. Such massively distributed identities have become almost as pervasive in industry as in religion. They are calculated to attract and to hold public attention. Here the symbol or trademark speaks for another collective group who seek to promote and particularize a family of offerings. Is it not strange that our near worship of free mercantile exchange is supplanting the morals once symbolized by a fish?

Yet, the individual still holds within his created personal symbols the opportunity for clarifying and giving significance to his own homegrown convictions. Certainly a widespread demand for such self expression, however minor, is evident in the ubiquitous gift shops selling emblazoned T-shirts. In our society of massive merchandising it is indeed irrational, to me, that we can select from literally hundreds of automobile models, each with its own identifying advertising emblem, yet we are almost never allowed to tailor a car, or much of anything else, to our own specific desires; except for placing monograms on car doors and stationery to match our silk underwear. Such paucity of creative expression makes the nostalgic mounting of cattle horns on the imitation Rolls Royce radiator of a Volkswagen "bug" seem almost prophetic.

Within a culture attempting to supply one of everything to everyone, it is apparently necessary to hold variations to a minimum. The individual cannot be allowed to require more than the signature of the group; the school tie, the fraternity pen, the mon, the club crest. Short of deposed royalty, or a rock star with a following, the only persons allowed a token of individual self expression, in our otherwise permissive culture, may be those of us with a registered cattle brand.

The creative activities carried on within our brains and stored in our memory must utilize coded symbols much like those that we can externalize and discuss here. Of course, the messages must be enormously complicated, more numerous and even more strident. These subconscious responses seem to have great difficulty in resolving disputes between themselves. For as we ponder a situation or analyze a scene there are dozens of recognizable and related symbols with each supported and further detailed by at least an equal number of shadowy variations. These conscious and subconscious abstractions of beliefs must be in a continuous state of ambivalence, transformation, and evolution. A tug of war between the seen and the sensed, the seeming and the known must be perpetual. Perhaps this constitutes the essential basis for curiosity itself. Each of our neurons must be constantly reevaluating new signals and speeding the coded results along to vacillating synapses where they obtrude and further permeate our overloaded indecision. Everything is equivocal and the resultant decision is never quite complete. The battle between reason and the synapting senses goes on.

As we make our percipient way down the length of the museum gallery or meander through the deprived streets of a foreign slum, an argosy of meanings, or symbols, surrounds us and are ready to spark a questioning mind. Those symbols within, whose existence we only surmise, must be communicating with those without that we recognize and partially comprehend. The strife to surface, to be understood through our conscious memory will persist, but the code that converts perceptions to memory can only come about through vicarious symbolism and searching effort.

As we compare the wide range of symbols that comprise our experience there are interesting natural contrasts and comparisons. Why do some of us prefer mountains and others seashores? Is it early training, accident, happy experiences or is it the hidden influences of our forebears? What are our personal symbols for mountain and seashore? How did they originate? What do they represent? Are our preferences based upon physiological make-up, mythological resonances, or psychological intuitions? Did we learn to like or dislike them or are such feelings simply innate?

Do mountains represent barriers to a desirable outer world or do they contain and protect our secret Shangri-la? Are they upheaving explosions or the making of future soil for fertile fields? Do they isolate and protect the independent cultures of the world or do they only make travel more difficult? Are they challenges that reach to the sky or only encumbrances between people? Do they represent collisions between continental plates or mere lecterns for past and future messiahs? Are they resources to be mined, pleasure domes for enjoyment, or only inconveniences to be accepted? Does the perpetual heaving and wearing between mountain and seashore represent primary natural forces or God's will? How do our visions differ between mountain ranges and seascapes? Is one the immovable object and the other the irresistible force? Is this how they are imprinted upon our thoughts? We know that both of these natural forces are essential, both are destructive, neither is benign, but how have they been associated within our memory of the past? Do we have a preference for one beyond the other? Why?

These seemingly irreconcilable but palpable feelings may not seem capable of resolution, yet such widely recognized, if diverse conditions, as mountains and seashores, within themselves, carry a mystique and historic symbolism that is peculiarly their own. We do not know how such feelings develop within us, but through our efforts to interpret such comparative symbols and figurative explanations they can be isolated and identified. We can then move forward to consider the viability of man, empirically or by way of classic Greek legends, for both extremes should always lie in the background of our thoughts.

It seems to me that the process of identifying such personal feelings underlies our fascination with visual interpretations and graphic meanings. Our desire to experience the unknown, to travel, to qualitatively record our feelings through visual reflections, at moments in time, all support our search for personal truth. As the shutter of our camera snaps open and then closed we reveal our experiential values and record much about out inner selves.

V   CONSCIOUS COMPARISONS AND CONTRASTS

The symbols that guide our actions and depict our values are not accidental. The process that we use to recognize and weigh these emblems of belief is of great consequence for they depict our inner feelings and allow fleeting insights to be retained and recombined. A chain of reasoning is little more than the linkage of these symbols of past decisions; a series of coded recollections knitting together earlier beliefs. The ongoing process of recognizing and evaluating these symbolic images demands keen observation and careful analysis. The character of each of these judgments alters those that follow.

Making use of comparisons and contrasts is an essential method by which we screen information. To compare and to contrast are different, but they are related acts in our search for greater meaning. By contrasting visual images, physical objects, and mental constructions we seek relationships that emphasize differences rather than simply revealing similarities. Later in comparing the same images, objects or conceptions we emphasize their alikeness. While we can examine similarities and differences by both contrast and comparison, we largely emphasize differences through contrasts and similarities with comparison. To contrast is to weigh with respect to differences while to compare is to view the object of concern in relation to another for the purpose of showing, or measuring, either difference or similarity.

As we mentally scan visual images and physical objects our memory must adopt certain representative symbols. These precognitions are achieved, it seems to me, through continuous comparisons with what we have already digested and accommodated within our memory. If the similarity or dissimilarity is significant we then expose this perception to a series of contrasts to see whether the differences are sufficient to alter the symbols that we already have in mental storage.

The only method for conducting a full cerebral search must be through the use of such applied comparisons. The new apprehension is thus passed before all of our previously stored knowledge to determine its substance. If found sufficient the new insight is contrasted with earlier truths, one-by-one, and if the sum of effective differences is significant a new abstract and coded symbol is subconsciously assigned to it for future recall. This symbol is isolated for future use, earlier beliefs are discarded, and all of this is done almost automatically, largely below the level of consciousness, through the use of representational memory fixes.

How we weigh and come to final conclusions is a mysterious act. How do we explain what we do and do not remember? How are our proclivities shaped? What gives us our sense of importance, our moral values, our hopes for the future? What is our sense of reason beyond mere personal preference? Why do we hunger for some things and ignore others? We know that the answers to all of these questions can only be found through logical comparison and careful contrast. The methods that the mind uses within; the measuring, weighing, balancing, analyzing and judging all rest upon what we have previously perceived; our capacity for reason and our conscious and continuing application of comparison and contrast.

All of our analogies utilize comparison and contrast. The thought that if two or more things agree with one another in one or more ways, then they will probably agree in other respects, is the basis of analogy. The possibility of this conjunction, in new ways and for new purposes, is our real workshop for ideas. Reasoning by analogy, apparently first made popular by Aristotle, rests heavily upon comparison and contrast. New combinations, seemingly incoherent when viewed separately, come together differently when paired or in groups; the variations and inconsistencies then seem to couple, and fresh possibilities emerge. Originally implausible and absurd, these concurrences are reshaped by another set of relations, an original force. Contradictions can become advantages as totally new concatenations occur. Long standing differences are usefully applied to support novel and original possibilities.

By comparing similarities and then contrasting significant differences, analogous opportunities appear. New relations, between what originally seemed to be unlike things, can produce objects and ideas having functions that reinforce one another and produce highly different results. Comparing the ridiculous and the inappropriate with the somber and the accepted is often mysteriously rewarding. Plumbers' methods are used to repair human hearts, plaster casts become chair bottoms, and the most mundane of human tasks produce ideas that beget Nobel Prizes.

As comparisons and contrasts are unlimited so are the surprises that unexpected combinations generate. It is the capacity to subconsciously perceive harmonious relations, between dissimilar things, that separates inventors from usual men. Apparently these gifted interlopers have a subliminal capacity to relate non sequiturs. Their abilities to observe, to extract essentials, and then to logically recombine seemingly dissimilar attributes must underlie their creative powers.

Growth is a matter of perpetual readjustment. In really seeing anything for the first time our entire body of knowledge and accepted truth, is subject to change. If interpreted with thinking eyes, a trip to the zoo may alter our religious beliefs or explain exogamy. Exposure to the Himalayan highlands allows us to understand the Louisiana swamps in new ways. Open air, rickety shacks built up the slope of a mountain may be found superior to multistory, granite sheathed apartment buildings on Fifth Avenue. Our deepest values are shown in our simplest decisions and represented within the brain by their personal symbols that we cultivate throughout our lifetime. The popular does not necessarily signify the true. In the United States, 250 million people often seem to be quite wrong. The most corrupt of prejudices, the thoughtless acceptance of public opinion, whether from biblical teachings or ethnic conglomerates, can only warp our beliefs when blind compliance is not balanced against our own independent experience.

In the photographs that follow, a wide variety of comparisons and contrasts of quite different visual sequences will be shown. Some of the views will be discussed; however hundreds of other comparisons are available for the reader's personal interpretation. By analyzing the significance of each photograph, by standing alone, we can compare what is to what might be. The reader can compare life to death, love to hate, sculpture to boats, sheltered childhoods to the viscissitudes of age, eroded pastures to verdant farmlands, clouds to mountains; what we see to how we see it, the permanence of mountains to a wisp of smoke.

Our response to these most generalized contrasts is influenced by heredity, tokens of the past, environmental changes, and the mechanics of our brain. How we choose to interpret what we see and how well we understand what we believe is of transcendent importance. These day-to-day, almost accidental perceptions, recorded as symbols in our memory, actually make us what we are. In the end we can be no more than the preferences that our eyes and minds have chosen to adopt; to be compliant or sui generis. A lifetime of wide-ranging comparison and contrast determines our conscious feelings, directs many of our preferences and influence our tastes. It is through a growing ability to choose between extremes that we educe change within ourselves.

VI SUBCONSCIOUS TASTES AND FEELINGS

Personal preferences grow from many sources. Some, those we achieve through reason and conscious activities such as comparison and contrast can be isolated. Others, less understood and more mercurial, are located below the conscious level of our mind-memory. We control our conscious choices but cannot be sure that we control what goes on within our subconscious mind. We are often helpless before these unknown forces. Preferences largely formed within the subconscious should connote better choices, but this is not always the case and they are not easily, or rationally, explained. We simply know that we like some things more than others. We are unable to stop and compare our rational decisions with the vague subconscious feelings that often shape our preferences. We do not usually analyze our predispositions or the reason that our mindset has taken a certain cant. We may realize a tendency, hold a liking, or adhere to a belief, but our reasons are seldom really clear. The process we choose cannot be improved unless we adopt the practice of dissecting the constituent parts, and relative value, of our day-to-day opinions. The forces of unexplained habit and repetition are certain to continue until we investigate our preferences and inclinations in a regulated way.

It may be possible to give some guidance to our subterranean mental processes by isolating specific situations and then carefully analyzing them. While lifelong accumulations of subconscious prehensions, habit, and reinforcement can outweigh a few thoughtful analyses, this effort to understand seems to be our only way to influence the powerful forces of our subconscious mind-memory. The threshold between our conscious world and the mythos of our subconscious experiences rests upon the active use of our five senses and, hopefully, a capacity to reason.

The sensibilities that support our tastes and feelings apparently occur from a mode of cognitive functioning that does not require conscious awareness. While the messages from the outside world are transmitted to us through our five senses they do not always seem to be associated with conscious mental responses or to enter our controllable memory. The messages are inserted into our subconscious as an immediate result of indefinite body feelings or are aroused by a form of endopsychic activity that we do not understand.

Tastes and feelings, the potent forces that influence and are influenced by unconscious mental activities, are usually as incomprehensible as the terms from which they are derived. These two sensual terms are imprecise and not subject to an accurate description. For instance, who can really describe the taste of a cantaloupe or the feeling of a loved one's death? We know that the terms are based upon prehensions that establish distinctive qualities and preferences but they are not undergirded by conscious reason. Tastes and feelings are not measurable and they are not limited to rational appraisal or appreciation. Even their origins are shrouded in mystery. These subtle awarenesses are the target of most advertisers, where messages are only meant to attract attention and a superficial emotional response that is not really understood.

The sense of touch, probably the first cause of feelings, must have originated to describe the sensation of nerve endings in the skin. The meaning has been enlarged, from the original perception, to include a vastly generalized group of sensibilities. As now used, the term extends from organic sensations to aesthetic responses. Feelings have been enlarged to encompass "the undifferentiated background of one's awareness considered apart from any identifiable sensation, perception, or thought." The word's comprehensiveness is only limited to "one's awareness," "one's emotional responsiveness," or to one's "capacity to feel emotion." The meaning of feelings, like taste, has been so expanded and generalized that the word has little real utility. We can exchange feelings for taste and taste for feelings, but in using the terms we will only be understood during the tipsy gallery opening.

The mass of awareness stored just below our threshold of conscious thought and often referred to by such words as taste, feelings, and inclinations influences many of our opinions. These almost automatic accumulations of generalized preferences are often the final test of our reasoning. After we have considered and studied any decision we usually retreat to the subconscious and allow our instinctually accumulated feelings and abridged experiences to decide the final outcome. Whatever we choose to call the terminal phase of any personal evaluation, whether delight, response, or qualitative essence, it is almost always sensually immeasurable, such as why music pleases the ear and love reassures. Our final response is almost always the result of these illusive inner feelings.

The triggers within that allows us to alter preferences, tastes and feelings are not consciously manipulable. They affect changes while we are unsure of their existence. Obviously, a great part of the deciding mechanism developed throughout a lifetime is not available for conscious use. These powerful and persuasive forces are only revealed through disassociated events. However, occurring just below our threshold of conscious reason these mental activities may be controllable at a level lying beyond normal consciousness. These metaphysical forces may respond to higher levels of industry, ego, and desire, or they may only be influenced through accident and repetition. We can call these subliminal forces.

Subliminal influences, or forces, do not produce a conscious or predictable response or sensation. They are seemingly insignificant and too weak to allow apparent discrimination; however, they influence our subconscious mind and act as triggers for change. Advertisers have long recognized the power of message flashes that occur with stroboscopic intermittency and speed. These almost instantaneous messages are received, sorted, and stored, within each individual, somewhere beyond conscious awareness. As with light, their lingering effects must be additive and grow in strength for they eventually alter our attitudes and ideas. Like ice below the waterline of an iceberg, they support all of our opinions. They constitute a large part of our entire personality.

These subliminal influences are apprehended through all of our sensate responses. Our daily experiences combine conscious and subconscious reactions. Some are recorded as perceptions, where reason can associate them with precedents, while others can only be applied automatically or through endopsychic accident. The methods that we use to edit and enlarge these liminal awarenesses are not understood but they obviously exist. The relations between conscious thought and these intangible tendencies must be quite complex and are certainly a recognized part of the creative genius. These uncontrollable natural inclinations almost always combine with the intellect to shape thoughts and ideas never before realized.

Our body of subconscious and instinctive awareness has at times in the past been misinterpreted and badly used. Obviously most formal religions give unreasonable credence to such recondite and abstruse sources of human action. Theosophy, anagogy, obeah, voodoo, and fashion advertising all deal with vague "inner psychic forces." We have all been told that deities and demons promise mystic individual salvation to those who will allow others to interpret their futures. It seem paradoxical that we could sublimate our individual potentials for life-enhancing growth for such absurd promises, simply because we do not yet understand the relationship between our subconscious prehensions and rational thought.

The merchandiser and promoter realize that most of our purchasing decisions ultimately involve subconscious feelings. Upon introspection, our likes and tastes may at first seem rational, but pursuing the matter further usually reveals that such arcane constituents as fashion, vogue and style were decisive in our final decision to make a purchase. Our mercantile leaders, having supplanted the religious ones, are using the same methods and recognitions as before. "Voodoo Economics" and merchandising misuse our vital subconscious impulses by deforming our sense of reason. Our appetites are daily groomed with subliminal half-truths so that we accept feelings for information and fashion for need.

The general acceptance of fashion as a prevailing custom is now more widespread than ever before. Television, radio, telephone, newspaper and magazine are everywhere and all are wired to the same central economic controls. Fashions and appetites are created overnight by simply submerging all opinion in a sea of similarities. Only a nonconformist bastard, usually illiterate and immune to word-of-mouth, can face such overpowering persuasion and reject such appeals. How else can we explain why we pay the same for a liter of flavored water as for the same amount of nutritious natural milk that requires many times more labor and months of expensive animal gestation. The needs of our mercentile markets cannot long tolerate such irrationalities. Only immeasurable tastes and unbridled appetites can justify our universal lack of buying logic.

The manipulator of public opinion is adept at intertwining conscious and subconscious awarenesses. He flatters our social sensibility and collective subconscious by using methods that could never convince the thinking individual. These masters of deception consolidate strong emotions and weak product to create a sense of immediacy, turmoil and need. They supply the public with either stimuli or mental narcotics to achieve the desired levels of love, hate and desire. They know that strong feelings are never quite rational. Who of us has seen a rational method of comparison and contrast presented by a selling advertiser? How many of us take the time to look, to understand, and then to buy thoughtfully?

Our dependence upon unrecognized awarenesses must result from psychic damage. As reason is less used, atrophy sets in and our subconscious mechanisms for decision making assume greater importance. Reason is destroyed by inaction and instinctual impulses and habit slowly takes its place. A chain of abnormality and irrationality occurs. The primary disorder brought on by lazily ignoring reason and replacing it with illusory beliefs produces slovenly reasoning and a vicious cycle of degeneration begins.

Many years later I acutely remember the odor of my aunt's Ivory soap kitchen. It is a pleasant, conscious recollection, my only remembrance of the time and physical environment. But, even as this thought occurs I know that dozens of other unconscious associations spilled into my subconscious memory. I cannot list these impressions but a generalized awareness permeates my recollections and I know that my aunt's kitchen influenced by entire life. Many of my tastes and intimate feelings must have had their beginnings in this place. A liking of Ivory soap undoubtedly began here but I also believe that a more pervasive need for psychological warmth also originated here.

Through the years diffuse associations, habits and routines are responsible for building our conscious memory and subconscious awareness. This bifurcation of our mind and its mechanisms is troubling. I know that neither aspect of my mind can exist alone and while I feel that they communicate, I do not understand any of the process. One part is easily imposed upon while the other apparently imposes. My awarenesses, my inclinations have few defenses but my conscious mind can be altered by the forces of logic and reason. This mental duality is not weighted but like the division of the sexes each of the two parts has esssential characteristics not present in the other. Our best hope for growth is to recognize nize these intrinsic differences as opposites, or at least as opposing associates, and while we may look and listen intently to the siren's call of potentially deceptive preferences we must authenticate our decisions through serious deliberation.

VII COMPREHENSIVE MYOPIA

Our perennial search for wholeness is never simple in this mercurial and astigmatic world. The duality of human nature, the conflicting polarities of our conscious and subconscious selves, and the interior-exterior aspects of understanding are difficult to resolve. We are driven by unreconciled forces as we search to comprehend contradictory human traits. We are, within ourselves, always divided, always seeking an illusive wholeness. Yet a deeper, even more unresolvable issue arises. Within the sentient human, is it possible to achieve a unitary whole, or are we endowed with the perpetual necessity of existing in at least two parts? Must we accept ceaseless inner conflict or are resolutions possible?

We simultaneously occupy inner and outer worlds. Do these worlds reinforce and strengthen one another as they struggle for ascendency? Does this consanguinity of parts, this separation of central powers, help or hinder our search for wholeness? Do rational comparisons compromise sensual feelings as transient tastes offer new interpretations of old beliefs? As we seek balance in our search for underlying truth must we use compensating opposites to find needed equilibrium? Do the forces acting within us require the counterpoise of an opposing set of external forces, or are they redundant?

A few pages earlier we considered the importance of using rational methods for making comparisons and contrasts and then juxtaposed this procedure against the less understood power of intuition. Who can say that one if always superior to the other? Each involves truth seen from different vantage points. Because it is more defensible we seem to believe that objective reason is superior to subjective intuition; however if intuition is built upon a summary of earlier experiences, even when not understood, it may at times contain greater validity than the power of cool-headed, but isolated, calculation. One side of this ongoing equation may only serve as a catalyst for action by the other. After all, the stabilizing gyroscope is composed of a wheel spinning about opposing axes. Perhaps our mental apparatus requires equivalent forces that act in opposition to one another.

Intuitive forces, seemingly acting automatically from within, are not measurable while objective reason can be appraised from without. Is this apparent advantage always real? We already know that quantitative issues are measurable while qualitative issues are not. What then is the measure of love, freedom, hate and joy, to say nothing of pain? Wealth is accumulated through calculable activities. Love and creativity cannot be measured and predicted. Neither can I alter my feelings regarding the music of my youth.

The polarities within our perpetually dualistic nature divide many of our attitudes into opposing camps. Seeking wholeness, we must accept the existence of these deep divisions. We all hold and protect a personal world, within, while exhibiting a more publicly acceptable universe without. One part is seeking to develop and explore a personal understanding of the part while the other attempts to combine the parts into an acceptable whole. The world within is a microcosm of accumulated feelings, a miniature existence where each of us is the epitome of all we know. The universe without is a macrocosm and involves a search for total understanding that combines great quantities, great truths, and great ignorance. We consist of a series of mutually exclusive dichotomies, for better or for worse.

The personal world within each of us requires constant enlargement. We dissect, segregate, and subdivide the known parts of the growing unknown. We use microscopes to inspect and understand the underlying order of the atom. We magnify the integral part and explore an unknown that becomes smaller and smaller. We study rocks to understand mountains. Solid state physicists analyze the very existence of matter itself in seeking to explore the foundations of the universe. They apparently believe that the whole can only be understood when the part is known.

The universe surrounding us insists that we aggregate known parts into a comprehensible whole. Through reason the large and unknown are reduced to smaller more understandable parts with estimated values assigned to each. The units are multiplied, enlarged, and related to others. We reduce the parts so that they can be coherently assembled and compared to other assemblies. We use a diverging lens, the reducing glass, to achieve a workable diminution of size and complexity. Astronomers seek the origin of the beginning, the foundation of the universe, for they apparently believe that the part can only be fully understood when the whole is known. They study black holes to comprehend infinity.

The microcosm, seeking a comprehension of the part, and the macrocosm, seeking a coherency of the whole, represent divergent views of a single concern. They look at the same objects from different ends of the same long telescope. Looking through the conventional eyepiece, the field of view is reduced while the objects seen are enlarged and made more complex. Greater detail becomes available. This is equivalent to a microcosm. Looking from the wrong end of the same telescope the field of view is greatly increased but the objects seen become smaller, simpler, and more easily grasped. This is equivalent to a macrocosm. The microscope is usually used to study the microcosm and the intellectual reducing glass to analyze the macrocosm. They ultimately show the same things but in different ways and from quite different points of reference. Either used alone is limited and distorts. The challenge, the resolution of this duality, lies within each of us as we pass through our challenging daily routines. To achieve lasting effect our activities must necessarily involve a myopic concentration of effort, similar to those of the physicist or the astronomer, but our life objectives must be more comprehensive, more hyperopic, as we attempt the resolution of all that we can know.

As we go about our daily lives and try to interpret the many types of visual images that confront us it is important to understand the growing bifurcation of these ever present polarities. They exist in many ways and because of their complex contradictions we are tempted to oversimplify and accept the popular black-or-white unitary answer. We do not choose to look at both sides of the tossed coin. The dialectics of comparison and choice are simply too difficult. Contradictory arguments and logical disputation seem unnecessarily time consuming. The multiplicity of answers emanating from two such interacting forces, often two opposites, are simply not worth the effort. Disputation can be left to the specialist.

The specialist, however, is generally someone who confines his interests. His qualities are restrictive and deal with limited particulars, not wider applications. The generalist, on the other hand, devotes himself to many concerns and only limits his activities to compressing knowledge into general laws. His concern is comprehensive applicability, not limited particulars.

So it seems that each deals with only a portion of human concern. A specialist has traits that can be described as myopic or shortsighted; the generalist as hyperopic of farsighted. One performs in concentrated, close-up depth while the other seeks wider and more diffuse insights. One concentrates effort to locate and originate while the other weighs and evaluates such new beginnings. Each represents only a part of the required whole.

It has been said that a shadow "is the only visible non-material thing in the world," but so is a mirror image. Dogmatic truths are dangerous to enunciate, but I do believe that the opposing forces represented by dualities and polarities serve us well in ascertaining the validity of dubious premises. As example, the comprehensive act of rationally assembling and assimilating permits wide-ranging accountability but it cannot originate. This is done by the lonely myopic seeker who reaches beyond his capacity and known reason. The myopic romantic is essential to the comprehensive rationalist, and vice versa. One originates and the other organizes and usefully applies. So it is that opposites are necessary to the welfare of one another and to the whole person.

To achieve an adequately balanced view of the world, to find wholeness, demands a fuller understanding of the real significance of what is seen. The view must be considered from differing vantage points. A balanced comprehension requires that we consider the bias of the myopic view as well as the more wide-ranging vision of the generalist.

VIII CHARACTER AND COMPOSITION

In developing a capacity to see what we like it is necessary to always balance the specialist's myopic vision against the wider interests of the generalist. To explore this seeming conundrum two words have been selected to illustrate the void that lies between such visual interpretations. *Character* and *composition* contain within their accepted uses a number of meanings that will hopefully introduce the reader to another facet of seeing with more acuteness.

Both of these very instructive words are widely used within all branches of the visual arts. If they were removed from the vernacular, easel painters, graphic designers and architects would find communication difficult. They span several disciplines and are essential in the discussion of visual scenes and images. *Character*, it seems to me, deals more directly with origins, ideas and distinguishing quality, while *composition* concerns communication, application and arrangement.

Character demands an essential identity, the intellectual value and unity of a thing, while composition asks for no more than a resulting response, a proper management of the parts. Character is primarily associated with moral values and the intellect, while composition serves pleasurable responses and sensual appetites. In gauging the substance of a scene, character describes values within, while composition defines appearances without. One has greater substance and is more difficult to comprehend, while the other has an easy appeal and is more obvious. In determining the character of a visual image, or thing, we must first find its wholeness, its unity, and its reason for being. In appraising the composition of the same visual image, or thing, we are chiefly concerned with how it affects our feelings.

In furthering our understanding of these descriptive terms it is well to know that the meaning of character originated as a symbol of distinctive quality, a mark indicating a special characteristic. Composition, on the other hand, suggests the manner in which something is composed or compounded, and pertains to a particular arrangement or combination of constituents. Composition indicates how something is put together, and here our determination moves from general principles to particulars. Character conversely, begins with an effort to appraise quality, define a thing's particulars and culminate in a comprehensive essence. Composition, it seems to me, is the way in which something is made to give an appearance that is free from disturbance or agitation. Composition moves from the general to the particular while character starts with particulars and combines them to find a greater, more comprehensive substance.

The character of a photograph, a building, or a person defines its intrinsic quality while its composition can only reveal the relationship of parts, the correctness of order and proportion. The effects of composition are superficial and extrinsic.

Character is the driving force, the intention, that intelligence uses to delineate a peculiar essence. Character is a conventionalized symbol that stands for distinctive quality and decisive will. A scene, a building, a person, can all express character in different ways but purpose, perseverance and uniqueness should be evident. Clarity of purpose and lack of pretensions should be inherent in the character of an outhouse, a racing yacht, or a wrinkled octogenarian.

Character transcends the vagaries of likes and dislikes regarding the arrangement of a composition. The intentions of a decisive will cannot be equated with tranquil organization or harmonious adjustments. Character can be calm and accepting but it must reveal its essential purpose.

Composition expresses a wide range of thought, good or evil; however, composition is a following and not an originating act. It is a means of communication and should be attributed no greater substance. We are told that there are standards of composition that can serve for thoughtful comparison and departure, but such standards can represent no more than ingenious manipulations.

In the mythological world of cult criticism and art historians such sublime revelations are only equaled by the dull tomes describing the shine on the Mona Lisa's nose or the angels dancing in her eyes. The apparent social necessity of such simplistic certitudes and classic credibility has been with us since the Romans plagiarized the Greek orders. Periodically society seems to return to the recondite nostalgia and thoughtless replication of earlier uses and their predictive consequences. The rules of Vitruvius, Vignola and Ruskin, when examined in detail, show that our futures have been intermittently sucked in to such cataclysms of the past. Character with its quality standards and arduous new beginnings is forgotten in the raging torrents and siren songs of such provocative and absurd compositional myths.

It is interesting that in its beginnings and within the archaic law of the Franks and Goths that "composition" was the name given to the sum of money paid for a wrong or for a personal injury, by the aggressor, to the injured party. This too was apparently "the ordering or arranging of something into its proper proportion or relation" and is measured by its order of correctness, not by its contributive substance.

In summary, the term character defines the aggregate qualities of a person, or the values contained within a thing created by a person, that distinguish them from their contemporaries. It should be noted that character depends upon distinctive personal characteristics, while reputation is based upon the traits that others believe one possesses. The constituents of character are clear and intelligible in relation to the whole person, view or thing. It is clarity of intention and moral purpose that most succinctly depicts character. In an object it represents the refusal of the maker to compromise the substance of the work, to accept the average, the commonplace.

The term composition connotes congruity, or an arrangement that subordinates the part to the whole: an artistic work whose various elements are combined aesthetically, usually through a sense of composure. Composition should enhance understanding and readibility for it can be no more than a vehicle for transforming the ideas and substance that lie within.

Proceeding with this explanation of how we should look to see what we might properly like, a number of other symbolic words and phrases come to mind. Their interpretations vary widely between individuals, disciplines and applications. To assume any uniform understanding between such terms as recognition and apperception, between music and poetry, sculpture and buildings, words and drawings, may be expecting too much. It is difficult to span these ranges of discrimination. In sections to follow such terms as space, time, mass, shape and form will be explored, but first I want to briefly discuss the sun, light and shadow and to speculate upon truths that we have so long taken for granted. Without light there can be no sight. The source of all light on earth, the sun, has always been man's transcendent symbol of ultimate power, life and hope. Primative religions that associated God and the sun, as equals, were as near truth as we are today. Whether origin or agent, the sun controls us all.

IX SUN, LIGHT, AND SHADOW

The sun is the source of all earthy energy. An intuitive understanding of this fact, known as "the light of life," apparently resides in the beginning of all religions. Even today more people probably worship the sun than any mythological man-like being. A greater understanding of the sun's character makes it no less dominant in our conceptions than it was in Ptolemaic Egypt when it was worshipped as a luminous celestial body and as one of the seven planets revolving about the earth. This star, ninety-three million miles away and around which the planets are held in orbit, is solely responsible for human existence. The sun is large, with over three hundred thousand times more mass than our earth. Is it any wonder that the winged disc of the Egyptian sun god and countless other ancient religions included emblems of the sun?

The electromagnetic radiation given off by the sun includes both energy and matter. This solar radiation is emitted in an enormous variety of wave lengths such as X-rays, gamma rays, ultraviolet, infrared, radio and visible light rays that travel at a speed of 186,000 miles per hour. Only a small fraction of these total wave lengths stimulate nerve ending in the humans retina and are therefore seen and called visible light rays.

That portion of the solar electromagnetic radiation that we receive as a sense impression in the eye, whether considered as wave motion or as a beam of fast moving particles, can be called light. Described as wave action the height of the wave indicates intensity, brightness, luminosity, or radiating light. The length of the wave, or the distance between crests, describes color, while the angular orientation of the crests defines polarization. The longest wave length is red while the shortest is violet or purple, royal colors.

Visible light, other than that received directly from the sun, includes: fluorescence, the glow discharge by a substance of electromagnetic radiation during the absorption of radiation from some source; incandescence, the emission due to physiological processes of chemical, friction, or electrical action; and iridescence, not an actual light source but the reflection of rainbow-like structural colors and shifting patterns due to interference in a thin film, or diffraction of light, due to the angle of illumination. Common examples of these include the fluorescent light tube, the incandescent light bulb, the luminescent firefly, and the iridescent colors seen on a soap bubble or some butterfly's wings and exotic bird's feathers. Each has distinctive properties beyond the capacity of the human eye to perceive. Colors seen under each of these conditions tend to be interpreted differently by the eye. Here, it should be noted that light colors and pigment colors mix and are perceived very differently. For instance, when red and green light sources are mixed the resulting color if a bright yellow. When red and green pigments are mixed the resulting color is a muddy brown.

Ambient, diffuse, and luminous light are related terms that should be understood to discuss the relative aspects of each. Ambient light surrounds, encompasses, envelops, and is suffused on all sides; while diffuse light is not localized but is distributed and spread freely. Luminous light is a steady light that is reflected or produced within. During the day a heavily overcast skydome might be described as producing ambient or diffuse light. Luminous light would be more like that produced by a luminous watch dial; however, luminosity describes the efficiency of radiation, quality of light or brightness. A bright light infers a high degree of radiating light.

Light makes vision possible. It is usually reflected from the surfaces of the object seen. All light energy originates from the sun but can be stored for long periods of time in other forms. In seeing properly, it is important to recognize the many variations and inconsistencies of light sources. Discriminating between such variations as light absorption and refraction is reflected by our interpretation of everything that we see.

The shielding of light, the lack of direct access from the source, creates relative levels of darkness. The area protected from direct light, for instance, can be said to be in shade or shadow. A surface, such as a wall, that is not in direct sunlight is in shade while the reflected image, seemingly projected on the ground or other surface, is a shadow. As stated earlier, the shadow, like mirror images, is a visible but non-material thing. It has been said to be a form from which the substance has departed. The primary human value of shade and shadow, when combined with texture and color, allows a much greater understanding of shape, depth, scale and time. To reduce potential confusion later, the shading of color is achieved by adding black, while tinting of color is done by adding white. A shade can also be a cover used to protect something from direct light.

Without shading and shadows sloping and rounded surfaces would not be recognizable in real life and would be impossible to depict in two dimensional drawings and photographs. Without light there is no color; with reduced light as within shade and shadow, color is altered. It can be said that colors are darkened when light is reduced, as when shading occurs because black is added to a pigment.

Generated by the sun, conveyed as sunlight, supplemented by shading and shadows, and supported by material reflections the conditions supporting sight are processed by the eye. The response in the retina to reflected light is conveyed to the visual cortex by the optic nerve and the process of visual perception and adaptation begins. The eye adjusts itself to the luminous environment as the brain directs it through the oculomotor nerve. In bright light it makes adjustments such as narrowing the pupillary opening. As light is reduced the pupil dilates and retinal sensitivity increases. These responses can be further adapted for observing two dimensional objects in alternative ways. By squinting, closing the eyes and then holding them wide open, we can observe quite different ocular aspects of the same object even under otherwise identical conditions. The object remains as it was but through such manipulations of our own optics we are able to alter what we see. We may thus choose momentary illusion or variation of our own making.

We sometimes think of illusions as misleading but it is not necessarily an attempt to deceive, distort, or give false impressions if we intentionally use such tactics with foreknowledge. We can simply squint our eyes and lift our head in a certain way in lieu of using a reducing glass. A mirage on the other hand is a distorting optical phenomena whereby we see such things as a quiet body of water on the horizon in the midst of a hot desert. This is due to a layer of heated air that causes light rays falling upon it to bend backward, creating a distorted displacement. Incoherent reflections such as this are distortions that we recognize. There are many others that we do not. The most damaging create misinterpretations and misuse. They do not always involve light or the eye. They occur as shadows within the conscious brain itself. They are misplaced beliefs.

However, what is a misplaced belief in one person may be an exquisite beginning in another. The sun is a universal reality while our visual world is composed of a combination of both light and shadow. Shade and shadow clarify what might be a mirage of sameness and make our interpretation of light, as it is reflected from things, understandable. As there is black and white there is light and as we look to really see, we must be conscious of both.

In Indonesia, particularly in Bali, The Wayang puppets create two dimensional, moving silhouettes. They are made of leather and designed to cast shadows of mythological figures upon a two dimensional white surface. Because of their very limitations these shadow messages are unusually powerful. It is this limitation and reversal of customary sight and color that so strongly reinforces the message. It is the white paper in watercolors and the black accents in photographs that underlie the strongest or most subtle messages. Either color or limited black and white are capable of equally powerful statements concerning our visual world.

X   SPACE, TIME, AND MASS

Space, time and mass are fully understood by ten year olds but unabashedly confusing to mature mathematicians. The words demand an understanding of infinity and the distance between classroom desks. It is impossible to discuss the most commonplace situation without some comprehension of their relations, yet their inferred applications are beyond everyone's grasp. These three words are necessary to describe the solar system and our own backyard.

For centuries space and time were understood to define separate and distinct entities. Space implied the lapse between two points in time while time meant a period during which something, such as an action, process or condition existed. The "space of time" and "a period of time" meant about the same thing, the experience of duration. Time was thought of as a "fixed and anticipated period of existence," a number giving space between two events. Time representing human need, was based upon experience, the possibility of repetition, and the need for predictability. Time was usually thought to flow smoothly from past, to present, to future. The scales that were used to measure time were arbitrary, whether solar, atomic or dynamic.

Space, has been defined as a limited extension of one, two or three dimensions that is bounded in some manner; a line of limited length, a line enclosing a space, or a three dimensional volume; a distance, an area, a volume, each with the abstract potential of extension or enlargement. In another sense space is the region beyond the earth's atmosphere; a three dimensional volume that extends in all directions without limit; a visualized condition of three dimensional space, containing physical bodies where the space would continue even if all the bodies were eliminated.

Aristotle postulated that time was "the numerable aspect of motion," while Immanuel Kant believed that time can only exist within the human mind, "a subjective mode in which phenomena appear." Until a few decades ago time represented the finite duration of the material universe, in distinction to the belief of unlimited duration, or infinity.

Early in the Twentieth Century the mathematician and physicist Henri Poincaré conceived the principle of relativity and postulated that no velocity could exceed the speed of light. A decade later Albert Einstein developed an explanation of the relative nature of time and space, in gravitational terms. Based upon the premise of simultaneity it was aduced that *time is private to each celestial body and there can be no single cosmic order.* Simultaneity simply does not exist with regard to time. Two events can be separated by two kinds of interval. One can be distance in space and the other a lapse of time. If two bodies, like the sun and the earth, are in relative motion there is no physical distance between the bodies at a given time. Time is private to each body and this is why either space or time is meaningless when standing alone under such circumstances. Space and time can only exist together as space-time. Space-time is a continuum with both time-like and space-like attributes.

Poincaré, and later Einstein, altered our understanding of the universe, perhaps comparably to the Copernican revelation three hundred fifty years earlier that destroyed the religious myth that the earth was the center of the solar system. As Copernicus planted the seeds of modern astronomy he may also have destroyed the myth of any self centered uniformity. A general acceptance of the relativity of the universe and space-time could produce even more profound changes of thought. A theory of chaos could even evolve.

The Theory of Relativity brings us to the third aspect of our verbal triad. Mass is an aggregation, a quantity of matter held together, a lump, usually of indeterminate shape, the extent of a solid object or the amount of space that a body occupies. Mass is the quantity of matter in a body, without regard to volume or the pull of gravity upon it; the property of a body that is the measure of its inertia. Within the Theory of Relativity mass is held to be non constant and to depend upon velocity.

In less esoteric usage, artistic and architectural space can be defined as the area within bounding lines shown by a drawing or painting, or the shaped volume delineated by sculptural elements. The representation, or effect, of three dimensional volumes shown within a painting can also be understandably referred to as space.

In like manner, time, within the arts usually refers to a specific time, year, or hour. It is the reflection of age, duration, or when represented, the fourth dimension. Time can be visualized as a division of geologic chronology, depicted as a warped clock face, or shown as the date stamp on an empty food can. In much common usage mass is the principal part of an object or an aggregate of all related parts. In building terms, mass describes the overall, three dimensional attributes of a structure's shape; a comparison of internal volumes as seen from the exterior.

Time, as the term is most generally understood, is fleeting and our visual images race forward in unlimited profusion. The visible world seems to literally explode with sensory images that the mind is incapable of accommodating. A very small portion of what is exposed to the retina is ever recorded by the brain. We apparently develop defensive mechanisms to prevent intellectual overload.

Our eyes continually sweep over wide expanses of view but are seldom brought to real attention. There is logical cause for this seeming deficiency. Our primordial instincts have evolved so that limited perceptions take precedence over deeper introspection and only these instinctual reactions authorize immediate mental responses. Our reaction is almost instantaneous to symbols of danger or imminent physical need but less pressing messages are largely ignored. Our normal view of our surroundings operates as though our eyes were wide angle lenses, out of focus to much of what they view. Only those things nominated by habit, specific prior instructions, or recent experience trigger the focusing device within our mind's eye.

Our intellect must sort out what is important before we can really see. This requires mental concentration and time. Because of this the drawing, the building, the photograph offer opportunities of lasting significance. They each record symbols of thoughts, plans, and conditions at a place in time. They stop action and permit a more thorough analysis. The kaleidoscopic images that might have overloaded the brain are now reduced to a single image, as though the moving film of visual action was edited to a single frame.

The majority of data fed into the brain through our eyes can be stopped and recorded by the camera. Space, time, and mass can now be reviewed in depth as we take the time to study these visual experiences as unified, composite configurations. The order underlying our understanding of the universe can now be interpreted through finite things. The coherency of the whole can be sought.

Whether photographs, buildings, or graphic designs, we can dissect and weigh the various components of space, time, and mass. Space can be considered as an area or volume that is set aside for a particular purpose. We can weigh the compatibility of space and purpose, actual space, pictorial space, dream and reality. Time can involve the finite duration of a creation's life, a judgment of established routine or periodicity, or simply the time of an occurrence. Mass can be related to shape and the potential aggregation of parts can be methodically considered.

The recording of images expands available time and often allows us to differentiate between illusion and reality. We lose the visual dynamism and variation that is so enhanced by moving the position of the eye, but in the exchange we obtain an opportunity for more deliberate assessments.

In the public mind mass is closely associated with shape but has little to do with form. Shape and form are carelessly and interchangeably used but form has a significance that shape does not. We must distinguish between such key verbal symbols if we are to fully develop our powers of observation.

XI SHAPE AND FORM

Much of life is committed to routine and repetition. Our only escape lies within our own curiosity. We must alter our view of life, our intentions, if we are to find greater variety and excitement. This demands persistence and a growing interest in commonplace objects and events. We must learn to look more precisely, to differentiate, and to make new judgments, and be willing to stand alone with our opinions. Some things, some places, some shapes are simply better than others. We must be able to say why they are better and then to act accordingly. When we do this everything that we see comes to represent an opportunity to improve upon what we thought earlier. Dull and conforming routine is replaced by new and exciting possibilities. Even the words that we use to describe our thoughts to ourselves become more precise and insightful.

We are told that societies always conform to general values regarding most of their acoutrements. Certainly ancient cultures adopted standardized customs, ornaments, and tools. Archaeologists uncovering the remains of the past expect their findings to confirm this pattern of consistent sameness. The mass of any culture's material possessions is much the same, as the vast storage rooms of our museums attest. Those who exhume articles from the past know that nonconforming artifacts are extremely rare. Whether caused by similarities of taste, limited curiosity, or simply by an acquiesence to convenience, we know that archaic societies have always produced a limited and usually trite range of products. The aristocratic sectors of a culture were more discerning but the bulk of the same society does not seem to have cared.

Even today we are surrounded by aimless artifacts of an endless sameness. Yet these recurring objects have a significant symbolic content. These are the objects that a millenium from now archaeologists will use to judge the state of our culture. The objects that we choose to live with will tell more about our real intentions and creative capacities than the written word. These everyday things reflect our values in an unequivocal language that leaves little room for ambiguity. We live with our tastes through free choices. The designer wearing a triangular faced wristwatch need not argue the merits of aesthetic reason.

In refining our individual design decisions two words are of supreme importance in discussing our perceptions. *Shape* and *form* are essential in both describing and appraising physical objects. In our time the description of an object becomes almost as important as the object itself. Unfortunately, like so many English-American words, the meanings of these two words seem to have proliferated aimlessly. They are no longer really meaningful. *Form* is particularly misued. It has come to mean many things. The form of geometric spaces, social graces, and perfunctory questionnaires all have equal validity. The properties of the word's logical use have nothing to do with its general acceptance, as we may surmise from the latest *Racing Form*.

The irrational interchangeability between the words *shape* and *form* does not allow their use in any significant discussion of creative design. To the designer, form should infer intellectual substance and idea. Shape cannot. Form should imply a participation in the evolution of human thought while shape can only describe externals. Form tells us the essential nature of a thing, as distinguished from the mere material of which it is made. Paraphrasing Aristotle we can say the "form is not shape but the shaping-force." Or, form is "the component of a thing that determines its position within its kind of species;" and it involves formal cause as distinguished from mere appearance. The form of a man-made object or building should revolve about the evaluation of an ideal, the real substance of a thing. Form presupposes character and is a shaping force.

In comparison, shape, to the thoughtful designer or critic, should only describe external appearances, usually one of a few recognizable geometric configurations. Shape, like space, may be of one, two, or three dimensions. Shape may suggest outline, mass, and body bulk, but it does not indicate the forces that made it as it is.

Form is a more complex and confounding term, which from the time of Plato has been used to describe the metaphysical aspect of objects and buildings. The transcendent idea, the universal essence of a creation is referred to as *shape*, but if intrinsic values, ideas, or the intellectual forces of change are at work, then *form* must be used.

Shapes are everywhere while forms, always created, are rare and more difficult to recognize. Form is the original cause of all manmade shapes. Forms, like ideas, always involve change because they are achieved through the application of human reason and creative powers.

The development of the automobile during the twentieth century allows an interesting analogy regarding the essential differences between the building of shapes and the conceiving of forms. As we drive along the highway we see endlessly similar shapes glide past. The only really identifiable differences consist of color and superficial stylistic sales nuances represented by annual models. They seem to be endlessly cast from the same mold. As a group, automobiles have identical characteristics and serve the same basic purposes. The minor variation that is discernable is intended more to satisfy the whimsy of the marketplace than to alter performance. Yet once in a great while a new form does occur and generates a new shape, to perform a new service, to meet newly recognized needs. In the last half century the jeep and the family van originated as such nonconforming shapes. In their beginning the essential nature of these vehicles was conceptually changed through the application of new values and ideas. These changes altered the vehicles' purposes and earlier shapes; and because of this created a form. A new kind, another specie, was born. The new jeeps and vans did much more than arbitrarily suggest new outlines, mass, bulk, and detail. They embodied a new ideal and essence. A new logic acknowledged need in new ways and this became the shaping force for a significantly different vehicle. The new form altered its kind and through a reinterpretation of needed performance created more than a new hybrid, that would in its turn allow the evolution of even newer forms. A certain method for distinguishing a form from a shape is to recognize that one contains a reproductive component that the other does not have. Man's evolving development is traced from form to form and it is the symbolic language of these germinal shapes that best reflects human progress.

In the two dimensional world of painting and drawing the separation of meaning between the words shape and form becomes even more complex, for here the families of shapes can be reasonably grouped but the families of potential forms seem to be infinite. As we seek to distinguish ideas, to establish essences, there are few basic guidelines. Shapes can be firmly grouped but forms are relative and only measurable in a general way. With forms the exception always makes the rule.

Because of popular usage the word *form* is quite abstruse in painting. It can mean the relationship between parts that are intuitively structured by the artist or it can simply indicate a technique. Here, it is necessary to recognize the difference between form, the verb, and form, the noun. Previous discussion has been limited to an interpretation of forms and shapes as nouns that define what is and what is not "a form," in physical objects. As a verb, "to form" means to frame, conduct, make, fashion, and so on, but the process of such actions may, or may not, result in the making of a form, a noun! The noun and the verb should be used quite differently, and with extreme care.

As we appraise the merits of photographs and scenes we must learn to distinguish between those that represent new seed ideas and those that do not. Within our frames of visual reference, shapes and sizes demand that we discriminate between such words as *shape* and *form* and scale and proportion.

XII   SCALE AND PROPORTION

Scale and proportion often overlap and the terms seem to even contradict one another for they represent some of the same things in very different ways. Both are concerned with relationships and relative sizes and both depend upon ratios. When we analyze the *scale* of a manmade object, such as a building, the ratio concerns the relative size of the human body and its parts to the structure and its parts. When interpreting drawings of the same object the relative size of the drawing to the full size of the original represents *scale*. Here, the draftsman and the cartographer use a ratio between distances drawn on paper and actual distances realized on the surface of the object or of the earth.

In the future it will be interesting to see whether the change from the British system of measure to the metric system will alter the scale and proportion of buildings and artifacts. The basic unit of one system was founded upon the length of the human foot while the other is based upon the more abstract length of a meter. The mature human foot allows the user a convenient and always ready reference for estimation. The meter is not related to the user's immediate anatomy and is therefore less comprehensible. The lack of such a simple relationship will alter future buildings and artifacts. Nature provided us with fingers (digits) and feet and such ready associations have enormous value. Unfortunately, these systems do not appear to be easily interchangeable today. Perhaps the evil began with dividing the unit foot into twelfths, thereby making fractions necessary. Zeros and decimals are much simpler to calculate, but they are not directly associated with the measure of the human body and therefore with visual scale.

We can use ratios to interpret or regulate the proportion of the parts of a thing; to one another and to the whole, but we cannot give undue credibility to the aesthetic satisfaction of the results. The search for abstract beauty of proportion has gone on for thousands of years and a number of thoughtful if limiting systems have proven interesting, but a universal acceptability has not been found. Emerson wrote: "The love of beauty is mainly the love of measure and proportion," while Edmund Burke rejected the conventional relationship between proportion and human beauty as caused "either by custom, or the idea of utility." Vignola and LeCorbusier, two paragons of aesthetic virtue, living centuries apart, developed systems of building proportions suggesting almost universal applicability; however, over time they have been found equally wanting. A universal guide for aesthetic proportions does not now seem attainable.

As we have already seen, scale and proportion while related can mean quite different things. The composer, designer, and statistician may generalize but the relationship between such disciplines is as different as the meaning of the words themselves. Scale to a composer and scale to a graphic designer may both involve measure, but what they measure is very different. The quality of sound and vision may be integrated within the brain, but they are not separately measurable in terms of one to the other. Their character is entirely different and only a third force such as the plotted curve of the mathematician will allow them to meet on common ground.

Proportion, while subjective in some respects, has many mathematical and graphic applications. The Pythagorean scale with its intervals regulated by mathematical ratios, rather than consonances and proportionate dimensions, relative to size, is of note. However, there must be an underlying and consistent guiding relationship or ratio, something that promises an eternal recurrence of things, such as classical Greek art or a rhythmical and measured beat of music. Proportion demands a congruous relationship of one thing to another and between two or more things. Beautiful proportions must contain proper portions relative to size and shape but these can seldom be mathematically predetermined. The essence of harmonious proportion is always qualitative and therefore is immeasurable.

In summary, scale is primarily a matter of comparison of sizes while proportion deals with desired relationships. The scale of something depends upon a method of measure associated with an understanding of the size of the human body. Vicarious scale can relate the human body to an intermediary such as a horse, an automobile, or a known feature of nature; however, the ultimate measure is always relative to the size of the human body. When we say "the scale of the surroundings" this assumes the size of the surroundings to the human body. Australia as a continent really has no scale for it is simply too large to compare to an abstract six foot tall human being.

Scale and proportion, two primary objectives of all classical art are founded in comparisons, relationships, and ratios. They are not illusions but do depend heavily upon current cultural attitudes regarding beauty. Normative ideals pertaining to scale and proportion apparently devolve from attitudes that never stabilize.

Shape and *scale* have received our attention alongside *form* and *proportion*. Our theory of relationships is beginning to combine *comparison* and *contrast* with *taste* and *feelings*. We have moved from conditions under which we see, by way of generalized shape and size and now wish to explore the exterior surfaces of what we see.

XIII   TEXTURE AND PATTERN

A scaly, scabby surface often produces a feeling of disgust. This apparently occurs because past associations subtly combine the sense of sight with the recollection of touch. Each sense is reinforced by the others. The sight of an object alone may be offensive but to see and to simultaneously touch or smell reinforces the repugnance. This compounding of sensual responses may underlie our reaction to such remotely related conditions as incised decoration on buildings or tattoos on human skin.

All of the light reflecting surfaces that allow us to see objects have texture, some more apparent than others. Materials have patterns that reveal their innermost composition, either visible with the naked eye or by enlargement. Texture and pattern are closely associated terms that affect such phenomena.

Texture generally reveals the identity of surfaces or material, their size, shape, and arrangement, such as the cellular appearance of a plant or the pores in human skin. Texture allows us to identify things by combining the visual and tactile surface characteristics of a material or shape. While texture can be seen and felt on the surface of objects it can only be represented by dark and light in photographs and drawings. Visual tactility, or the perception of texture without the ability to actually touch, can be represented through the use of surface shading, color, and tonality. George Braque, the painter, held the belief that the viewer and the object he viewed were separated by "tactile space" while objects are only separated by "visual space."

Pattern is almost always more precise and specific than texture since it represents the essence of a repetitive unit that permeates and organizes a thing. It occurs in the real world in such places as in photographs depicting the microscopic crystaline organization of specific materials, the whorls in fingerprints, or the scales on fish. Such patterns constitute a reliable basis for identification, either directly by the eye or through the microscope. Patterns are essential in both identifying and categorizing materials.

Routine and commonplace recognition and description can be achieved by identifying textures and shapes but more specific and precise determinations demand the greater detail found in patterns. Texture is usually visible from greater distances and is therefore recognized before pattern. Texture is described by the degree of external roughness while pattern demands more detailed examination and greater exactitude. Texture may be used to identify and distinguish the general characteristics of something but the innate nature of the basic structure and its composition can only be determined from its revealing pattern.

With manmade things pattern is based upon a recurring unit. This unit pattern is a matrix used to shape the structure of a larger vision, or the design organization for a work of art. Manmade patterns occur in such typical places as paving designs, bas reliefs, or the distribution of pellets from a shotgun.

The word texture seems to have originated from the weaving of fabrics where it was used to describe surface structure and tactility. The descriptive degrees of texture are quite limited, usually with two primary extremes such as: fine or coarse, smooth or rough, nobby or rugose, and for only very widely recognized conditions. Texture, based upon the roughness of the material, alters the reflection of light, is limited to surfaces, and is not necessarily intrinsic. This leads to the recognition that the term texture has gone beyond its original meaning and now includes such descriptions as the amount of fat in a steak, the chewiness of water chestnuts and the distribution of built shapes within a neighborhood. Usage has diluted and altered the word's more essential meaning.

To be able to interpret what we see we must depend upon the shape of objects and their external surfaces. One, without the other, makes a judgment difficult. For this reason drawings and photographs are often misleading. As example, except for scale, a photograph of frost crystals on a window can also be seen as a garden of tropical ferns. The skin pattern of the fruit of the Nut Palm looks very much the same as the back of a Scaly Anteater. Size, shape, color and other attributes must be combined with texture and pattern if a valid identification is to be made. The visual interpretation of a pattern often demands a great deal of additional information, for with patterns greater specificity is always possible. Texture essentially refers to tactility and surface identity and this can be visually represented through shading and shadows. Patterns incorporate structural differences that may appear visually the same but are as different as molecular structures and the topography of river basins.

Manmade patterns are often used to achieve a sense of visual depth, or roughness, through the use of shade and shadow. As an example, the alabaster screens enclosing the tombs of the Taj Mahal are carved with an interlaced design similar to fabrics. Prayer recesses in the Alhambra are adorned with lace-like Moorish screens, Arabic inscriptions and other geometric designs. Both are patterned to present an overall texture, from a distance, but when seen close-up they are also figurative. Here, elaborate patterns provide needed shade and shadow and physical coolness.

We are constantly exposed to mysteries of depth and distance. Our perceptions are greatly influenced by the way that objects reflect light. Without reflective surfaces depth and distance cannot be visually determined. Desert mirages and a forest in darkest night represent extremes of reflective environments. Accurate perception of depth and distance is impossible under either of these conditions. Our entire visual experience is based upon reflectivity and therefore the texture of surfaces.

The disorientation occasioned by a missing horizon cannot be greater than when a total loss of depth perception occurs. The estimated distances between the viewer and related objects control most of our response mechanisms. The very thought of a world limited to two dimensions is almost inconceivable. Repetitive pattern, including the microscopic composition of all matter, and texture, allowing us to generally recognize most shapes and surfaces, combine and create the visual environment in which we live.

An adequate visual environment has many attributes but few, if any, are more essential than the perception of shape, depth, and distance. A moving stream of measured motion can be created with repetitive patterns which we can also refer to as *rhythm*.

XIV RHYTHM AND COLOR

Derived from the Greek "rhythmos," rhythm can be defined as the recurrent alternation of strong or weak, large or small, rectangular or round elements within a stream of sound or sight. It includes the grouping of weaker elements about stronger ones. Rhythm is the compositional relationship of harmonious parts within an ordered sequence; a regular recurrence of similar features. Such rhythms occur in nature, music, dance, buildings, and in all types of artisitic communication. Rhythm presents various combinations of patterned successions in divisions of time, distance, space, and movement. All types of muscular coordination, including dance, athletics, and close-order military drill involve repetitive and rhythmic movements. It may be simple, symmetrical, regular and recurrent, as in a rhumba, or it can be an irregular serpentine wall but both must have regular accents in either time or distance. Alfred North Whitehead believed that "The essence of rhythm is the fusion of sameness and novelty; so that the whole never loses the essential unity of the pattern, while the parts exhibit the contrast arising from the novelty of the detail."

The relations between rhythm and color are many. Harsh sounds, disunity and strife can be expressed in music as dissonance and in graphic art through strong and even garish color contrasts. Discordant sounds are equivalent to clashing colors. Harmonious colors are readily associated with melodious music. We relate discords and dissonance, in music, with gaudy, florid, and antagonistic colors. Such discords and lack of harmony are expressed in contemporary music, painting, and buildings and justified as artistic communication.

There is probably no aspect of seeing that equals the importance of color in the human psyche. Color has always played an important role in human existence for it is capable of dictating moods, enhancing experience, and altering emotions. Color has been used to symbolize victory and defeat, life and death, evil and good, but not necessarily in the same way. In occidental tradition white represents life, hope, and purity but in some oriental traditions it symbolizes death.

We recognize that rhythmic changes of color occur throughout the year. The monochromatic winter scene is gradually supplanted and emblazened with the colorful brilliance of spring; which in turn is subdued as bright greens darken into summer tones; then make the gaudy transition to the fall colors of yellow, red and gold; until the full cycle of winter with its gray and colorless values returns. Yet many of us let these rhythms of light and color pass unnoticed. We simply take such conditions for granted. Most viewers do not really see color but only sense it through the haze of a darkend screen. They reserve their attention and understanding of pure color for photographic images and their limited contrasts and precise edges. A real appreciation of the beauty of nature's colors, with their graduations and subtle tones, is unusual.

Our lives are immersed in color and unless asleep or forcefully diverted color serves as an essential stimulant in everything that we do. Because color is so pervasive we seldom recognize its full impact upon our lives. A simple demonstration of our lack of color awareness is to look through the ground glass of a reflex camera. The limited, but identical view upon the viewing screen seems so much stronger and more urgently brilliant than the same scene seen with the naked eyes a moment earlier. A superficial analysis tells us that the black frame, surrounding the limited view on the ground glass, produces a strong contrast with the brilliant color. Our natural vision, to the contrary, gradually drifts away at the edges into a soft peripheral focus. The view in the ground glass, much like that of a photograph, is of a size that lets our eyes respond to a clear and precise image of colors, within the essential limits of the frame.

The retinas of our eyes have a central depression, the macula lutea, and within this depression an even smaller area of most acute vision, known as the fovea centralis. The fovea covers an area of vision limited to a cone shaped opening of one degree. At a distance of three feet it allows us to see objects equivalent to the small blood vessels in the eye, wrinkles around the eye and details such as pores in the skin. The macula allows an acute area of vision that at a distance of three feet covers an area of about one and a half by six inches.

When light is reflected from an object into the eyes it activates color cones in the retina and a perception of color occurs. Color, as noted earlier, is a property of light that depends upon various wave lengths. When light strikes a colored object some of it is absorbed and some is reflected as a different wave length. A black surface absorbs all wave lengths and a white surface reflects all wave lengths. The three primary colors of light are red, green and blue. The three primary colors of pigment are red, yellow and blue. Light is additive and therefore if all three primary light colors are combined the result is white light.

When pigments are mixed the resulting visual sensations differ from those of pure colored light. The process is referred to as subtractive because absorption of some of the color wave lengths of light occurs within the reflecting pigment itself.

When we see a red object we know that the surface of the object absorbed all but the longest wavelengths and therefore the color of red is left; or the red light, with its long wavelengths, was reflected from a neutral surface, or a combination of these events occurred. Color results from combinations of pigments and light and lets us differentiate between objects otherwise appearing identical in size, shape and texture.

The potential for color to record and alter human emotions has been recognized throughout human history but little remains to tell us how it was actually applied. A few pottery shards here, a faded burial fabric there and a very limited number of discolored murals are all that remains to record thousands of years of human effort. Dress, household furnishings, and color applied to surfaces for psychological and emotional effects have been lost through time and exposure. Even where color was applied to stone or metal sculpture and lasting building materials it has faded into uninterpretable shades. It was not until the Renaissance and the invention of perspective that murals and easel paintings, as they have been woven into our written history, came to record our color preferences. Since the Renaissance however our spatial concepts and psychological responses to color have been recorded in brilliant and evocative hues. With the advent of widespread color printing during the last few decades color has reached even more deeply into our human psyche. Universal color printing has profoundly altered our basic visual values.

As you view the following photographs it is important to relate your personal preferences to the many facets of color, rhythm, and the other aspects of seeing that are so cursorily covered here. Among others, the outlook and position of the viewer should be given thoughtful consideration.

XV   OUTLOOK AND PERSPECTIVE

When asked to define the word "materialism" during a Princeton design conference Susanne Langer curtly responded that she never discussed words with "ism" endings. The required generalizations and logical shortcuts were apparently too great; yet, a few months later I found on the cover of a softback copy of her *Philosophy in a New Key* the statement: "*A Study in the Symbolism of Reason, Rite, and Art.*" Apparently her "isms" had to be just right, so I shall commence this discussion with my understanding of the word *perspectivism*. It has been defined as "a concept of philosophy: the world forms a complex of interacting interpretive processes in which every entity views every entity and event from an orientation peculiar to itself." Perhaps Ms. Langer's snippy response was relatively correct after all! As I use the word here it involves the conscious process of mentally weighing and then testing different visual outlooks, until a decision is reached that satisfies out inner self.

This includes placing yourself, the view, and the scene in relation to fixed points of reference. This can be referred to as orientation, a term that allows the viewer to manipulate positions, angles and associations. Proper perspective, or outlook, allows the viewer a sense of stability and purpose. The viewer's relationships are determined by the comprehensive arrangement. At this certain moment and place the viewer is the center of the universe and the molder of ultimate reality. The location should be significant to place, time, event, and viewer. It is special unto itself; it is momentarily at least sui generis.

People from distinct cultures and milieus differ in many respects beyond language, ethnicity and religion. They see and relate to the space that surrounds them in distinct ways. Their sensory backgrounds vary and they perceive the world in unique ways. Advantages are weighed upon separate scales and bodily preferences interpreted in separate ways. Across the earth we live in highly different, often antagonistic environments.

With the advent of instantaneous communication the world seems to be acquiescing to the belief that there can be only one overriding rule of truth and propriety. There is less and less room for curious, idiosyncratic, individual beliefs and nonconforming points of view. We are unctuously told that we must look at the same things in the same ways, whether it be automobiles, the death penalty, or our newest local office building.

We are even told what to look for and from where to view it. Very soon all reputable art museums will have footprints inlaid in their floors to give us the only proper viewing position. LeCorbusier, always challenging his time, built an assymetrical precolumbian pyramid adjacent to the Ronchamps Pilgrimage Chapel to furnish the proper viewing position for his sculptural masterpiece. Such superior vantage points, or lookouts, should not be arbitrary but supported by personal reason. Each of us should develop logical explanations and be able to explain why we looked as we did.

Each of us must search within ourselves for our reasons, the origins of our habits and superstitions. Why, for instance do we commonly accept "up" as good and "down" as evil? From ancient times, even though caves were protective, most societies feared the underworld and revered more exposed and hazardous heights. In Greek mythology darkest evil was ruled by Hades and darkness while the word "hell" apparently grew from Norse and Anglo Saxon myths. Muslims think of hell as a place within a concentric crater and Hindus conceive of twenty-one hells below the nether world. Buddhists have eight hot hells and eight cold hells in Kamacavara. Why is hell always thought to be down and heaven always up?

Middle eastern mythology is riddled with the mysteries of height and its powers for good. Whether shrouded with fleecy clouds or bathed in oceans, the mystique of mountain heights consume Hellenic Greece and other pre-Christian thought. Mt. Olympus, the home of the gods in Greek mythology, Mt. Ararat, the legendary landing place of the Ark, and Mt. Sinai, the legendary origin and lightning filled ambience of the ten commandments all involve mountain tops. Why is height such a prevading and forceful component in so many religious episodes? Does it merely let us relate to the surrounding horizon and feel the stimulation of being at the center of the world; or is it the reassurance of boundaries that we seek as we outwardly view the universe? If so, why would not a cave guarantee us greater psychological security?

Does our reverence and awe for the mountain top, or the highest place of immediate experience, have a simpler explanation? Does the visual perspective from such high places give us the capacity to view the world below for its more remote relations, or does simply seeing greater distance lend us a sense of power, a feeling of godship? Perhaps such elemental revelations reaffirm the reason for our primative beliefs that God is up and the high places have sanctity.

The way that we look and what we see has a great deal to do with our predispositions, what we believed, before we looked. Prior thoughts also severely alter what we see. The position that the viewer assumes before looking often produces predictable responses. Obviously, we are more likely to receive happy and optimistic sensations from a sunny mountain top than from a dark mine shaft.

From such sublime thoughts we must descend to the more finite aspects of ocular measure. In finding ways to appraise visual vantage points we must consider human anatomy. Angle of view and clarity are related to the construction of the eye, its lens, retina, and neurological relations, as well as to our everyday habits. Such phenomena as the fact that our eyes are located five and a half feet above walking surfaces and that recognition involves moving the eyes up-and-down rather than from side-to-side must be considered as we investigate our potential for seeing. Mentioned earlier, the fovea centralis is a small area within the retina that allows maximum acuity of vision. The macula lutea, the central depression surrounding the fovea centralis accommodates an angle of view of about twelve degrees in the horizontal and three degrees, vertical. Reading and detail inspection utilize these areas of refined retinal distinction. When scanning greater distances the horizontal angle of vision varies from ten to sixty degrees. The vertical angle of vision is also about sixty degrees. For our generalized purposes we can say that we have a normal cone of comfortable vision of about sixty degrees, vertical and horizontal.

Since our eyes are about five and a half feet above the ground the vertical limit of the eye to a horizontal plane gauges how far back we must stand from an object to be able to see the entire image in one glance. The old rule of thumb that we should stand twice as far away from an object as it is tall is based upon such factors. This rubric does not include the vertical movement of the head, and it should be noted that our horizontal peripheral vision, with eye rotation, can be as much as one hundred eighty degrees, with focus unclear at the edges.

These generalized comments regarding our physical limits of seeing reinforce the advantages of an elevated outlook. The view, or perspective from the top of Mt. Everest, at over twenty-nine thousand feet above sea level, must be overpowering. By simply standing taller we can enlarge our understanding and this may partially explain the mythology of the ancients. To this we must add the psychological mystique of difficult ascents, cooler temperatures, wind, and cloud movements and changes in the barometric pressure.

Such oversimplified explanations of visual phenomena can be misleading. They comingle the physical and psychological aspects of seeing and a very small change in one can drastically alter the other. Such rules of thumb are good for estimates but dangerous for precise applications.

Drawings and photographs are useful in showing various aspects of things but we must know that by their very nature they cannot be completely true and accurate. Methods used in making such images are based upon focal lengths, picture planes, and vanishing points that do not actually occur in nature; however, such assumptions help us discuss our perceptions. This is why the differences between drawings and photographs is so instructive.

One of the definitions of perspective is the "art of delineating solid objects upon a plane surface." A perspective view is one in which the observer's eye is placed at a point where all projecting lines originate. According to Leonardo da Vinci "linear perspective has to do with the function of the lines of sight, proving by measurement how much smaller is the second object than the first and the third than the second, and so on until the limit of things seen." Linear perspective is a purely geometric system where everything is seen from a single point of view, or outlook. The image presented on a plane surface shows the apparent relationship of objects as the eyes roughly see them in space.

The origins of perspective drawing are attributed to the painter Uccello and the architects Brunelleschi and Alberti and originated in the fifteenth century. Foreshortening, a related artistic development recognizes the depth of drawn objects. Depth and distance are shown in two dimensional drawings in a number of ways other than through the use of perspective. The relative size of objects, lineality, height, detail, composition, shading, and other heirarchies were all used before the invention of perspective drawing to indicate depth, distance, and the space between objects. The occidental conception of space emphasizes the distance between things, while in Japan the spaces themselves have meaning. The Japanese are deeply conscious of the shape and arrangement of spaces and the "ma," the criteria underlying the design of their gardens, becomes a sought-after harmonious spirit. The visual results are similar to the magnificent sense of space and direction found in precolumbian ceremonial complexes such as Panenque, in Mexico, and Copan, in Honduras.

Perspective drawings may have from one to several vanishing points, where visual rays, or lines of sight, converge. Even so three dimensions cannot be drawn with complete visual accuracy. The drawn line never duplicates the subtlety of the directly seen image even though the relationship between carefully drawn linear perspectives and photography can be very close. Geometrically projected perspectives and photographs, taken through normal lenses, assume symmetry about both vertical and horizontal axes. The human eye does not. The angles of camera view available in most interchangeable lens systems vary from 1,000 mm

lenses with 2.5 degree cones of view, to the 16 mm lens with its 180 degree plane of view. The angle of view of the 1,000 mm lens lies between the angles of the macula lutea and the fovea centralis. The 16 mm lens has an angle of view that is much the same as our eyes' horizontal limit of peripheral vision.

It is the 35 mm lens, with its 63 degree angle of view that allows us to stand at twice the distance of the height of the object to be photographed and take a picture of the entire object. This lens is actually quite similar to our own eyes, in this respect.

As we look the scene may change. The powers of variation that are built into our sensing mechanisms are infinite. The brain, in interpreting these on-going visual messages is in a state of continuous flux. Time and space interact with fact and preference. We see the same things differently by season, time of day, sex, and those always unknown forces of preference. We have the capacity to choose, to magnify the microcosm or to reduce the macrocosm; to choose the static, where everything stands still, or the dynamic where objects enlarge as we approach and diminish as we depart. We may look up or down, above or below, and within or without. We can assign values to these attitudes and choose between dark episodes and bright events. The psychiatrist or the psychologist can be our guide or we can simply seek to find for ourselves. In the search to understand what lies within us such apparently bland and mundane sequences as how we look at trees or sense the mass of a mountain may show us new potentials for productive living.

Our outlook on life consists of much more than our material surroundings but a continuing personal analysis of our immediate physical world will provide us with insights beyond our expectations. The ability to perceive the macrocosm of human existence form the microcosm of our immediate lives, even trashy back yards, is determined by each of us. This is the essence underlying "The Birdman of Alcatraz," the flowerbox in the window of a West Virginia coal miner's cabin, and great scientific insights.

Given a great panoramic overview, a moment of drama, or the climactic action of a Superbowl, most viewers group together to see the popular and the predictable in conventional ways; however, now and then there is the nonconformist, the potential creator, who stands to one side, out of the crowd and traffic, and attempts to see the truly unusual. Within the theatre audience there is usually someone, perhaps the producer of the play itself, who finds the audience reaction more interesting and informative than the dramatically constructed moment; or the sportsman who feels the terrible defeat of the unused quarterback. Swimming against the current of surrounding opinion is seldom comfortable but history is largely altered by such people and the attitudes and perceptions that shaped them. So it is that as we look outward on life we should not feel fettered with the fear of not meeting society's acceptable way of seeing things. We can seek new perspectives, new visual methods, by merely looking a little closer, asking why, and wondering what might be.

Whatever perspective or perspectivism may mean, it is important for all of us to know that we live in a world that is both complex and interesting, where each of us can be different, see more, and develop an orientation peculiar to ourselves. This new view of life can begin with the resolve to better understand what we have always taken for granted, what we see.

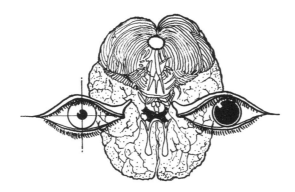

PART TWO: SEEING WHAT I LIKE

I AN INVENTORY OF PERSONAL PREFERENCES

To develop and further refine some of the visual criteria just described twenty thousand Kodachrome slides have been reduced to one hundred twenty photographs. The method used to bring about this reduction and to place the photographs within fourteen categories is briefly described in *Appendix A*. The selection process was performed over a period of several months but it must be admitted that the final results represent little more than personal preferences. Any justifications that appear in the following pages were composed long after the initial appraisal was made. All of the pictures were taken during fourteen years of travel.

The photographs are consecutively numbered as they are shown and discussed. In addition, each is shown on the List of Photographs, by categories, and is geographically located and dated as to when the photograph was taken. Each category will be discussed as an independent entity but on occasion related to the other groups. The reasons that I find each of these photographs important to me is, in the end, shrouded in mystery as I believe most things are that influence our deepest sensibilities.

Who can explain quality or beauty? Any really beautiful experience is always partially mysterious.

II CLOUDS

As a boy in Texas, before the arrival of the rice fields and the weeds, I remember the horizon encircling a virgin plane that went on forever. The earth looked the same in all directions as grass interspersed with Myrtle bushes stretched to the meeting of land and sky. Here the fascination started. The great skydome with its floating sentinels, overreaching even Texas, dominated the prairie below. These giant watchdogs of heaven were intimate daily companions. They foretold the weather and gave regular relief from the summer sun. As cloud shadows scudded across the great plains they vivified the ground-clinging plant growth, the birds and the grazing animals. The sky was vitally alive with changes that affected all life. The continuous movement of clouds dominated the world of sight and made ground-based activities seem trivial. The sky was larger than anyone and daily associations emphasized this truth. Clouds were the very essence of life as they made human existence worthwhile. Wordsworth to the contrary, clouds are never lonely, and neither are those humans who join with them on their journeys.

Working backwards is always subject to distortion but even today I know that my emotional life could not have developed without being able to look upward to the comforting sky with its friendly clouds. The pure blue of the desert sky does little for my psyche; however, the soft underside of a herd of cumulus friends sliding by elevates my spirits as little else can. I read their reassuring shapes and recognize only hope and a sense of freedom from their friendship. Their effortless and everchanging shapes occur out of nowhere, always an ultimate mystery.

Lying between heaven and earth as they do, clouds are perhaps the most elemental of the forces that shape our life on earth. Man's attitudes have been influenced by clouds throughout our time on earth, even though they have greatly changed through geologic time. They are undoubtedly changing still, even as they alter the weather and act as flagmen to warn us of seasonal variations. As they were once thought to house angels and gods, they are now appraised from outer space, categorized, and have their moods and movements explained by scholars ranging from astrologists to astrophysicists.

Some technicians think of clouds as little more than conveyances for moisture, as gigantic tank cars that arrange meetings between our great land and water masses. As there would be no power on earth without the sun, there would also be very little plant and animal life without these transient water sources. How feeble a Hoover Dam when compared to a cloud-season. Without them what deserts we would have. But, to the aircraft pilot clouds are more important as harbingers of change, wind direction, and weather. Clouds constitute the landscape of the sky and sometimes seem more human and mercurial in their acts and attitudes than the passing pilots. Like people, their shapes and families change and overlay one another. Clouds appear from nowhere and return the way they came. They lie at the heart of myth and reality.

Without clouds the Kalahari and Louisiana would be the same. Those waifs in the sky are of many types, levels, extent, and content, but they have one characteristic that is always present, they contain moisture as either rain, fog, mist, haze, sleet, hail, snow, or in combinations suspended within their seemingly aimless shapes. We see them daily, often several types within a few hours, but recognize few. Since primitive man, the attributes of clouds have been woven into our thought and social structure. They have been associated with both the high points of human accomplishment and with gross depravity. Floating on a cloud of happiness or under a stigmatic cloud of shame, the very term, cloud, has many connotations.

It may be this breadth of meaning, this very ambivalence, that creates the mystery in our minds that we call beauty. For clouds are closely associated with some of our most inherent human emotions. Through the analogies of the ages we have associated their powerful natural influences with both good and bad ranging from reclining angels to clouded logic; from religious cloudscapes of sublime harmony to violent thunderbolts emanating from deadly black clouds; and from uplifting thoughts to cloudy distortions. Apparently clouds can equally envelop angels and evil spirits or describe swarms of insects or uncertain speculation. Clouds can threaten and clouds can reassure, but it is almost impossible to reconstruct an exterior scene where clouds, their presence, intonation, and subjective symbolism has not altered our conception of time and place. Clouds are pervasive. In one of every five photographs shown here they are major contributors to the central effect.

In *Photo 1, Clouds Over the Pacific, 1989*, we see the wing of a plane skirting an enormous cumulonimbus "thunderhead." These beautiful and seemingly calm and billowing formations constitute an ultimate contradiction, much like peace and war. They appear gentle and soft on the outside but are more like a crazed animal within. These dense clouds can extend upwards to twice the height of Mr. Everest, and while their tops are a fleecy and happy white, their dark bases are merged with low ragged clouds that often contain lightning, down drafts, and hail. Cumulonimbus thunderheads are associated with tornados and waterspouts.

As we fly calmly above these objects of great beauty, it is well to consider their attitudes, both within and without, their external appearance of well being and their fuller potential for harm. We may admire their sculpted and fluctuating shapes, symbolic meaning and cycles of change, but their central significance to each of us is found in our own supporting experiences. Our infatuation with the cumulonimbus cloud could stem from remembering that hail stones over five inches in diameter have fallen from such clouds, or that a small plane mistakenly attempting to fly through such a cloud was so damaged by hail that it later appeared to have been attacked by hundreds of heavy hammer blows. As symbols of such memories photographs have great power.

In *Photo 1, Clouds Over the Pacific, 1989*, a sense of elemental power and ferocious strength is subjectively coupled to the diagonal thrust of the plane wing to produce a composition, a resplendent moment, where grim antagonists are in communion. The cloud's potential for destruction is contrasted with its calm demeanor. The adversaries are momentarily at peace.

Half a world away *Photo 2, Manaus to Salvador, Brazil, 1977*, is in strong opposition to *Photo 1*. A clear and happy understanding gives way to a confused foreboding. Instead of direct, bright sunshine a disorienting combination of oblique light, clouds, and reflections dominates the viewer's unusual position. Water, in its various states of suspension, creates a confusion of cloud types and even obscures the horizon itself. A visual disorientation, often so fatal to the aviator, creates a powerful response in the artistic observer. The composition of crossing diagonals is foiled by the brightness of sunlight reflected from the river's surface and the cumulus clouds floating above it. Distances are not ascertainable, and the viewer floats in illusory substance and reflection. Cirrus, cirrostratus, and cumulus clouds are related vertically and in depth. The river symbolizes the perennial transition from headwaters, to ocean, to sky, as it meanders toward infinity. The thin feather-like cirrus clouds dominate the skydome with their narrow bands and patches of ice crystals. The wisps exploding from the apparent visual collision of land, sky, and river are called "mare's tails." Combinations of such strong visual forces are often associated with the "cloud ring" that encircles the earth at the equator. Panoramas of this kind must be breathtaking for astronauts returning from outer space. The complexity of cloud recognition, as they seem to merge from one type to another, must generate an unsureness equivalent to reaccepting gravity and earthly existence. The museum of cloud formations shown in *Photo 2*, illustrates a relationship where land, water, and ether are joined and force the mind in several directions at one time. Here, nature is seen at its purest and scenes such as this must be indelibly inscribed in the psyches of all fliers.

Antiquity has many faces, but some of the most beautiful must be the remains of the Mayan culture found on Mexico's Yucatan Peninsula. Here for thousands of years men have built to their gods. The peninsula jutting out between the Caribbean Sea and the Bay of Campeche was once one of the most heavily populated areas on each. Mayan ceremonial ruins are everywhere. They are often covered with the growths of centuries and overriden much of the year with unbelievably beautiful cloud formations. Many people visit the Yucatan to re-explore the precolumbian ruins while others, knowingly or not, are drawn by the magnificent formations of winter cumulus clouds. They serve as ethereal foils for the sturdy stonework of the Maya.

Photo 3, Chichen Itza, Yucatan, Mexico, 1982, illustrates the colorful contrast between a vivacious sky and a somber earth. The entire area is arid and in constant need of rain, even as these great detached domes of moisture march steadily by. Both cumulus and stratocumulus cloud formations float past like chimerical dreams but produce no more rain than mirages in the desert. Again, desire and fulfillment approach one another, to the satisfaction of neither. However, to the visitor these sentinels lend needed shade and create lighting variations that allow a better understanding of space, time, and mass that the ancients' ceremonial centers used so well.

In the Himalaya mountains, two and a half miles higher than the Yucatan, the Kyichu River is surrounded by hills as it winds its way across a level plain. Almost totally devoid of plant growth, the sandy, desert-like surfaces surround the few small irrigated fields. The great white clouds pass in their splendor but drop little moisture. The summer afternoon sandstorms whip down the river valley to noisily paint adjacent mountainsides with the multicolored grit carried along in the wind's wake. Like the strokes of a giant paintbrush these colorful overlays emphasize the white clouds above.

Photo 4, Kyichu River near Lhasa, Tibet, 1988, expresses the essential trinity of land, water, and sky and emphasizes the significance of clouds.

The interactions of these three great constituents of our planet are exposed daily through the subtle exchange of colors at these high altitudes. The scope and the power of these perpetual forces influence something within our psyche that alters all of our aesthetic judgments.

Returning to nearer sea level, *Photo 5, Rio Negro, Manaus, Brazil, 1977*, shows a vibrant riverscape and its visual relations with a foreboding sky. Deep within a continental land mass the disorder of commerce is contrasted with the power of the anvil-shaped cumulonimbus cloud that dominates the horizon and human initiative. Conditions below obviously exist at the whim of nature's forces above. The frailty of human existence is evident.

III   MOUNTAINS

Riding the relatively recent and probably quite insignificant satellite earth, we do not understand or control the forces that lie within or below us, and we cannot remotely contemplate the indescribable powers that extend outward and above us. We do know that the earth's surface is in a state of continuous change, that great opposing forces cause land masses to crash into one another. One of the most obvious demonstrations of this is mountains, some still heaving upwards. We do know that the forces that create these gigantic wrinkles, or cones, are due to forces within. How these forces are related to the general movement of the earth and changes from without is still not understood. We only know that change is proceeding and we have no comprehension of its limits.

It was not until I was in college that I saw my first mountains on a trip to Monterey, Mexico. To a flatlander these heaves in the earth's surface were truly astonishing, magnetic. I sensed their power even when they were swathed in soft clouds, and I can still hear the reverberation of children's voices in the valleys. The echoes of laughter, the taunting slopes, the rounded masses often with crucifixes on top, challenged a new understanding. The unyielding stolidity of these enormous stone shapes was in complete contrast to the sensuous movement of the encompassing clouds. The mountain had staked-out a place on earth and patently intended to defend it forever, while the giddy clouds were always on a lark moving for the sheer joy of the dance. One was seemingly everlasting and the other everchanging.

But as all freshmen geologists know, mountains are made in several ways and they are in continuous change. They are made in three ways: by uplift, by erosion around an object, and by eruption. About twenty-five years ago the theory of continental drift began to gain acceptance. The crust and upper mantle of the earth's surface is much thicker under land masses than under oceans. Great land masses such as Gondwanaland that once incorporated large portions of South America, Africa, India, and Antarctica developed rifts that allowed the continents to separate, or escape, and for oceans to intervene. These prodigious movements may be triggered by volcanos. Some rifts, where plates are moving apart, are still active, such as those below the Red Sea and in the Gulf of Aden where the Africa and Somali plates are subject to rift faults. In other locations volcanos alone accumulate material to create mountains, such as the Hawaiian Islands.

The Himalayas are an example of mountains created over one hundred fifty million years ago by the prehistoric movement of gigantic drifting plates on the earth's crust and upper mantle. After their separation from Antarctica, what is now India and the Himalayas drifted northward where they collided with the south coast of Asia. The Indian landmass, moving northward, slid below the crust of the Asian landmass cutting off the top of the Indian crust to make what is now the Himalayas, and then continued to slide below the Asian crust due to the enormous weight of the Himalayas. Millions of years of erosion from the Himalayan Mountains have filled the trough created by the collision that created the Ganges and Indus river basins. The Tibetan plateau consists of the compressed remains of the original Asian crust while the Himalayas themselves are little more than an accretion of rocks and sediments shaved from the Indian landmass as it slid below the Asian plate. This explains why many of the mountain peaks are capped with sediments. The Himalayas are thought to be still growing, since the underlying plates on either side continue to push against one another. In contrast, the Andes Mountains in South America may be diminishing in height, because the horizontal forces that hold them in place are weakening.

These great geologic events have enormous influences upon all aspects of life on earth. Mountain ranges decisively alter rainfall. Clouds usually lose their moisture on the windward side of mountains, while the leeward side is arid. The Himalayas and the Andes are excellent examples. Tibet and Peru are very dry while India and Brazil have bountiful rainfall.

Mountains alter weather, but of equal significance to man they appear to determine human attitudes. Whether due to altitude, inaccessibility, or defensive advantages, mountain people have a long tradition of individuality, freedom of thought, and independence. While history records the societal accomplishments of the people of great river basins, it is well to remember that these basins begin within, or are surrounded by, mountains. Throughout history mountains have been incubators of freedom, whether in the Alps, Andes, Pyrenees, or Great Smokies. As a rule, mountain people do not seem to tolerate crowds for long periods of time, but choose to stand alone as individuals, or in small, select groups. They require greater freedom and solitude than other people.

In some respects the emotional attraction of mountains must be iconoclastic. Perhaps the advantages of gravity in archaic defense positions was decisive, but even today helicopter and satellite overviews have not lessened the mystique of mountain isolation. Even the sanctimonious urbanite, dictating rules to the world, has not been able to suppress this basic human sensibility. The cultural contrast between people accustomed to river valleys or to mountainsides can be extreme, because their value systems differ so greatly. Today we seem to have become a world requiring a uniform level of social compliance with the only possible escape from enforcement, as with moonshiners, in inaccessible places that have little economic value, demand great physical exertion, and no one else wants. Individualism, as generally interpreted today, has become a form of primitivism. As our technology and massive population overgrowth move relentlessly forward, it seems more and more likely that real freedom and self-determination, as we now know it, will not be possible, even in the most remote mountains. Our only future road to individual freedom and escape from massive collectivism may be to dig into the earth like moles to escape the pervading self-righteous, democratically-determined demands of a group-dominated society. It is not accidental that St. Matthew's Chapter V begins: "and seeing the multitude, he went up into the mountain." Today we are told that the people who love multitudes are the luckiest people!

It is strange that the word spirit, "a being having an incorporeal or immaterial nature," is so often associated with mountains and the emotions that they evoke. A basic contradiction seems evident. Mountains, the most physical, massive, somnolent, and inhuman objects known to man enter into the human psyche and can almost possess a person. Once adapted to their subtle influences, a person can never be really happy except in their presence. They become a simultaneous source of energy and renewal. Like spirit, mountains have a characteristic quality that overrides ordinary understanding. They represent the mysterious, the heroic, and the adventurous. Their imaginative emotional appeal stands tall and firm. They show themselves for what they are. Individual peaks lift their heads like giants, impervious to the steady assault of rain and erosion. Is it any wonder that they are given names and attributed human traits; that they are so cherished that they are sometimes even worshipped?

Mountains reveal much of their physiognomy from above, but depending upon the observer they wear many veils. Clouds, snow, plants, and shadows keep their mystery intact. *Photo 6, Himalaya Mountains, Chingdu to Lhasa, 1988*, is a glimpse through the cloud cover that seems to incessantly clothe these mountains. The snow caps feeding the central valley stream, that in turn flows into a green lake, forces our thoughts into conceptions much the same as James Hilton's Shangri-La in *Lost Horizon*. Mile after mile of snow covered peaks and inaccessible lost valleys emphasize the vastness, the overwhelming scale of the place. It was several years after World War II that the three highest peaks of the Himalaya-Karakoram range were climbed (Everest at 29,028 feet; K-2 or

Dapsang at 28,250 feet; and Kanchenjunga at 28,146 feet). This remote, high area of the earth is still little known to the outside world. These mountains' secrets are still untold.

Less spectacular, *Photo 7, Schwartberg Mountains, South Africa, 1981,* illustrates the subtleties of older mountains as they stretch into the distance only a few thousand feet above sea level. The words of Thomas Wolf, writing about the Appalachian Mountains of North Carolina come to mind as he said: "Ranges that melted away in purple mist." The lavender peaks in the distance convey an ethereal overlaying so subtle as to appear to be multiple camera exposures. In the late evening, when this picture was taken, the light moves rapidly as if nature were rationing the beauty of the moment. A few minutes later only a single profile remained.

Another delicacy of color occurs in *Photo 8, Yamdok Tso, Himalayas, Lhasa to Gyantze, Tibet, 1988,* in south central Tibet near Bhutan. Viewing the high plateau from several thousand feet above reveals the soft skinlike texture of the mountain sides, in contrast to the arid desert of the valley floor (except where the green of irrigated fields brings life to the blown sands). Here, almost three miles above sea level, the torturous road winds about lifeless surfaces. It is only the clouds, as their shadows constantly create new abstract shapes across the horizon, that let us know this is not truly the devil's playground but a highly visual environment where views change by the moment.

A few miles away *Photo 9, Mt. Kanchenjunga, Darjeeling, India, 1985,* illustrates another aspect of the Himalaya range. The photograph was taken from the extreme end of Observatory Hill; Buddhist temple bells were ringing in the background as the day awakened. The hovering mist and clouds, so much a part of the entire region, give the view greater romantic depth. The site is near the Darjeeling Mountaineering Institute where Tenzing Norgay, the Sherpa Guide who first scaled Mt. Everest, was teaching at the time. He made numerous attempts to climb Everest, lectured about his dearly beloved mountains, and died of a lung infection in 1986, thirty-three years after his final victorious assault. Listening to Tenzing and looking toward the mountains made me realize that they exist for yet another purpose: to teach climbers and hikers self-reliance, up where manmade rules have little significance, where the separation of mountain, weather, and lack of stamina can mean certain death. Mountains will always remain authoritative symbols, for in them there is no sham, only their inexplicable reality. The challenge, "because they are there," will always ring in the ears of youth.

By one definition a mountain must be over one thousand feet tall. *Photo 10, Sulawesi, Tarajaland, Indonesia, 1987,* shows a gentle and friendly old hill-mountain on a Celebes island in Indonesia. A few hours drive from Ujung Pandang this little prominence rears itself out of adjoining rice fields alongside the present day highway. It is out of place, but for some unexplained reason, when confronted by more dramatic,

well known, and unusual features this eroded mound stands out. Whether it was because these mountains were so unexpected on a relatively small island or because of something in my prehistory, I could not ignore a feeling that it represented something special. It could be the gentle way that it touches its surroundings or the way the reflected light is absorbed by the skin-like surface, or the farm tucked away at its spreading base, or the expectancy of the rain clouds at its summit. For some reason this mountain is as comfortable and unassuming as an old shoe. I recently read that beauty in human faces is simply based upon the law of averages. Our memory records dozens of faces and superimposes them upon one another. Beauty occurs where the most images fuse. Beauty too, according to this thesis, is based upon averages: one recollection is apparently worth only one vote in a properly reasoning mind.

The drama of great upthrusting rocks, though not mountains as such, can bring froth artistic responses equal to any sculpture by man. *Photo 11, Li River near Quilin, China, 1983,* is an extraordinary visual event. Slowly floating down the mirror-like river surface is a boating and visual experience without equal. Anthropomorphic, zoomorphic, and geometric shapes vie for attention as they pose with feathery bamboo, water buffalo, waterfront villages, and greenswards. Long workboats break the mirror finish of shoreward reflections as shades and shadows play with the miniature mountain shapes. While we passed in review, it seemed as if their natural profiles stood at attention, almost as people, too large for human creation but too small and idiosyncratic for real mountains, a lineup of personalities at the very edge of human understanding.

Reflections of cloud formations compete with the blurred and inverted images of distant mountains in *Photo 12, Lake Louise near Banff, Canada, 1988.* Virgin forests and sparkling water create a sublime setting for the humane scale of the Canadian Rockies near the Continental Divide. Like views from the surface of the Li River, middle distances are at work and should not be compared with the more expansive Himalayas. Here, the western Hiawatha speaks of continental virginity:

> "Through their palisades of pinetrees,
> And the thunder in the mountains,
> Whose innumerable echoes,
> Flap like eagles in their eyries;"

Photo 13, Copper Mine, Oquirrh Mountains, Utah, 1988, is taken of a North American plateau almost as high as that of Lhasa, Tibet. Even the colors have a similarity. Here a massive strip mining operation is slowly eating away the grandeur of nature but at the same time creating something equally allusive and powerful. The serpentine trails created by mechanical monsters leave abstract shapes even more exciting than the more human-scaled rice terraces of China and the Philippines. Seldom do the works of man seem to compliment their place on earth so well. Here, clouds and mountains meet the works of man and they embrace one another. After the passage of a thousand years the washed sensuousness of these gargantuan shapes will serve as a more lasting memorial than the sum of the copper extracted. In future ages, archaeologists may admiringly compare these ruins with other mysterious constructions of the past.

Mountains may be majestic, remote, or ominously poised. As they rear-up, or retreat, they can be seen as bulwarks against human aggression, as protection for the noncomformist. Their sinister enchantment can give way to a dreamlike beauty as light, seasons, and atmospheric changes occur. A frenzy of blinding snow can be quickly transformed into a romantic silvery mist. Mountains upon mountains can be obscured by clouds above, or enhanced by fog in the valleys below. Mountains, like men, are capable of many visages in quick succession. These visages should be thoughtfully interpreted. Grin or grimace, serenity or agitation, are interpretations that lie in the mind of the beholder, for mountains are as much spectacles for the mind as for the eye. The imagination of the beholder must react to their subtle variations.

IV   FOG-SMOKE-MIST

Nature constantly reforms itself, always following precedent but in a variety of ways. If we look we can see these variations. They are the cosmetics of nature. The same forces can dress a mountain or obscure a swamp. They can make seeing beautiful, or they can eliminate it.

Sunlight, moisture, and temperature constantly interact and, along with pressure, alter the way that we see things. These three constituents bring about our visual reality. Except for the cycle of day and night they are the most powerful influences for visual change that we know. Clouds and other modes of moisture suspended in the atmosphere create conditions allowing alternative moods because of changing levels of obscurity. The view of an apparently stable and static object is in fact a view in constant transition.

We know that warmer air holds more moisture than cooler air and that moisture condenses upon contact with a cooler surface. The temperature at which moisture condenses, that is, becomes water, is called the "dew point." Dew was once thought to fall from the heavens, but it actually occurs when moisture accumulates in small drops on a cool surface through condensation of water vapor in the surrounding air. This usually happens during the night following a hot day. Dew is most plentiful in the early morning. Robert Browning interpreted this phenomenon in *Pippa Passes*:

"The year's at the spring
And day's at the morn;
Morning's at seven;
The hill-side's dew-pearled;"

Surfaces change, reflections are altered, as an ethereal delicacy envelops the obliquely lighted early morning landscape. Warm air striking cool surfaces alters the way that we see the world.

The same phenomenon, or warmth meeting cold, in slight variation, creates both mist and fog. Mist is composed of an aggregation of minute water droplets occurring near the ground. At higher elevations, with less pressure, mists and clouds have essentially the same contents. They both exist as a vapor or water precipitated in smaller and more densely compacted units than that of rain. Mist can be distinguished from fog as being more transparent and made of drops that have a perceptible downward movement.

Vapor is diffused particulate matter and includes mist, fog, fumes, smoke, smog, haze, and steam that all involve critical pressure-temperatures between liquid and gaseous states. Many combinations occur but all involve the suspension of solid or liquid particles in the atmosphere.

All of these natural forces alter, becloud, or obliterate what we can see. They have each created their myths, responses, and special indulgences. People and places are often associated with such natural occurrences. Fog alone relates London and Sherlock Holmes, Calcutta and street sleepers, New Orleans and Voodoo. Excessive moisture suspended in the atmosphere limits and constricts the view, but at the same time magnifies the importance of what remains visible. Perceptions from within a dense mist or fog are much like those within a great translucent circus tent; the scene is limited and dramatized, the soft focus of what we see allows new mental images and serves to stimulate new, if puzzling, sensations. Such obscurations can also alter perceptions by emphasizing a certain aspect or, like a theater curtain, by enhancing the excitement of things yet visible.

The soft and largely gentle transitions through which we are allowed to view different aspects of the world each have their deeper significance and proper application. The atmosphere that we look through, and take for granted, alters the way that we see and feel. Sunny spring mornings and foggy fall nights are within themselves uninterpretable yet our differing feelings about such contrasts alter the way in which we later view life. Every type of day or night has some advantages over the others. Each is enigmatic and inscrutable except for the values that we place upon them within ourselves.

Mist, fog, spray, and smoke serve varying visual tasks and create different emotional responses. In *Photo 14, Mountain Clouds, Karimabad to Khunjerab Pass, Pakistan, 1989*, the clouds create a soft ceiling, directing the view downward to emphasize the enormity of the river valley. They relate the intransigent scale to the permanence of the Karakoram Mountains, but they also imply the presence of powerful forces that weather, erode, and change. The misty clouds are completely impersonal and of inhuman scale, but they animate a chain of mountains. They are caring, then uncaring, always changing.

Photo 15, Misty Road to Summit, Tiger Hill, Darjeeling, India, 1985, shows the interior view of comparable clouds and their very human associations. The mysterious and glowing light within a cloud, enshrouding a mountain road, creates a fragile stage for routine human acts. Brewing tea while waiting for the clouds to pass, the pilgrims trek up to a mountain top to see the sun cast its first light on Mt. Everest. The occasion is made even more memorable by such contrasts as this emission of a diffused light that comes from everywhere, surrounds the viewer, and seems to bathe the entire scene in a radiating glow. At the top, *Photo 16, Clouded Sunrise, Darjeeling, India, 1985,* the mist-filled cloud is less dense but still produces a glowing translucence that envelops the assemblage. The diffusion of light tangibly emitted from all sides dramatizes the participants as they anticipate the explosion of another sunrise. The sense of enclosure is as acute as if the sky were made of a fabric.

Photo 17, Yeats Memorial, Dublin, Ireland, 1977, divulges an early morning haze that emphasizes the low oblique angle of the rising sun and starkly silhouettes the surrounding shapes. The scattered light in the unclear distance contrasts with the intensity of the sun's rays as they strike the durable stones nearer the eye. The haze emphasizes the foreground and gives it unusual strength while the center of interest remains the misty distance beyond.

Fog is usually less transparent than mist and therefore creates compellingly inexplicable visual situations. Eerie relationships, particularly as they pertain to potential maritime activities, associate the danger of unexpected collision and drowning with poor visibility. Recording such conditions brings about immediate psychological responses. *Photo 18, Harbor Fog, Oslo, Norway, 1986,* makes the soft quiet of an early morning almost tangible. Odors are held to earth and intensified, sounds are magnified, a new impression of the world is at hand. Nearby colors are brightened while those farther away are lost in an ether of whiteness. Some objects are seen in stark detail while others blend into a universal background. The view is greatly limited and thereby intensified. Emphasis can be enhanced by limiting the capacity of the viewer to see. At such times visual loss can become an artistic advantage.

Another source of visual obfuscation, smoke, has a long history of human association. Man, the fire-making animal, has been physically and psychologically exposed to the burning of carbonaceous materials, with their visible residue of carbon particles, from the beginning. Deep emotional responses are obviously prevalent, as attested to by fireplaces in twentieth-floor Manhattan apartments and the ubiquitous barbeque pit in suburban backyards. Smoke mingles our present with our past, whether the cast iron backyard boiling pot of the frontier laundress or the stainless steel forks of summer-camp weinie roasts.

Photo 19, Smoke, Coba Ruins, Yucatan, Mexico, 1988, records an event of earlier times, whether the fall yard burning of small-town America or the spring clearing of prairie grazing lands. The morning sun slicing through the trees and casting fleeting shadows on both benign smoke and transient surfaces is movingly illusory and carries our thoughts backward to our elemental awakenings. Subconscious responses are revived through the unconscious imagery of fire used for pleasant human purposes. However, it is not warmth, utility, and brightness alone that strikes our innermost conscience; it is something more sublime, perhaps emanating from our earliest animal awakening, the magic of combustion. Fire, the gift of the gods and the uses we have made of it, must be continually reinterpreted by every sensitive human being.

Water, on the other hand, is fire's antithesis, its ultimate contrast. All of the things we have discussed here involve water in its varying conditions as it participates in our daily activities. The atmosphere that we breathe and through which we look contains water in many different states and densities; however, water's greatest importance is buried deep within our psyche. Whether downpour, fleeting cloud, soft fog, cutting mist, roaring waterfall, or tinkling trickle, water is our source of life, as fire has been our primary source for change.

Photos 20 and 21, Waterfalls, Iguacu, Brazil, 1977, confirm the power and wild abandon that can occur where geologic formations oppose the flow of a great river. Both photographs dramatize the relationship between water as a moving and visible liquid and as a first visible and then disappearing vapor. In one photograph the massive volume of falling water is not evident, even though the churning mist is; in the other, diminutive people stand on a flimsy observation platform to give scale to the place as they confront the fury of the deluge. The deafening sound and tremendous generation of fog-like mist completely dominates the distant and detailed views in both photographs. Primitive people have perceptively called such misting waterfalls "the smoke that thunders."

The decorative effects of water, as a liquid and in its many vaporous states, whether alone or mixed with other ingredients, is obvious. Our responses, whether to the soft, humid air of New Orleans or to the knifelike environment above the arctic circle are engrained in our psyches. Each of us has been prepared for our tastes and responses by earlier experiences. It is only through a concerted effort that we can break such psychological conditioning. The mystery of water and its omnipotent influence on our lives is firmly imbedded in our sensibilities. We have learned superstitions too: Dew is slick and poisonous to open sores; fog causes consumption; and marsh smog generates electrical storms.

44

Superstitions; too, arrive "on little cat feet."

The magical qualities of childhood mix superstition and substance. It is only later that we realize that the loss of this innocence, through the demands of conformity and economic survival, have endangered our appreciation of beauty itself. We cease to think, to really care. In later years we need to reeducate ourselves with respect to what is, and what is not, socially acceptable, what is beautiful and how we should proceed to satisfy our most guarded beliefs. The pristine, concise, and firmly focused statement is not enough. A layer of the unknown, the conjectural, the manifoldly interpretable, together with an opportunity to express our individual beliefs, are essential parts of both art and beauty. Compliance with custom and current artistic standards is not enough. We must individually decide what is beautiful and satisfying, and then ask ourselves "why?"

The most visually significant components of our living environment, such as clouds, mountains, fire, and water come in ever new combinations. Shapes and types change and are supported by thoughts borrowed from other sources. Yet we learn early in life that we must discern between black and white, good and bad. We categorize everything in such gross terms and learn, usually too late, that we have irreparably damaged our ability to gauge beauty because of such oversimplifications.

Apparently sometime in my past, sunlight, bright colors, and frothy white water came to represent happy events. Dark clouds, overcast days, muddy water, and slick stones at the water's edge came to denote moody and unhappy events. Such percolations from the past deserve new explorations as we attempt to refine our sense of beauty.

V   HAPPY WATER-MOODY WATER

Even viewed with clear and happy eyes the acts of nature are not always beautiful. They can be ominous, create fear, and leave a sense of foreboding. Our personal values allow us to separate good from evil, beautiful from ugly, and happy from moody. Our personal code of values should create relative ranks for making such determinations.

By thinking we seek to accommodate the new with the existing; reforming what we are by determining what we would like to be; and attempting to fit new perceptions to existing beliefs. For instance, as we deal with the more elemental aspects of nature we should group similar forces so that they are more manageable in the future.

What we call beauty, or beautiful, is the product of our thoughts as they enlarge our consciousness. What we see and the judgments that we make often subconsciously, serve as models for future action. We are conditioned by indecipherable forces that eventually create our value

system. Many of our decisions are subliminal, the result of such forces as hammering television and sales programs. In the spirit of our time we are told what is beautiful and desirable and we acquiesce to what is so blatantly forced upon us. Who can resist the permeating truth and purity of the Muppets or the Disney syndrome? Besides, "it is the healthy thing to do" and we can thereby escape any responsible thoughts of our own.

Ultimately, each of us is responsible for the values that we hold, whether representing individual, communal or societal points of view. Our values are a measure of our ultimate worth and reflect our own distinct character. Whether originating within the individual or only paraphrasing the acquiesence of a group, these principles and standards guide our lives. Taken as a whole our personal values direct our future purposes. Our values, our hopes, and our worth are much the same.

The recognition of beauty, a sensation that gives us happiness, that expands our understanding and vitalizes life is difficult to understand and to control. The things that we believe are beautiful should appeal to our whole being, our senses, our intellect, our experience, our anatomy, everything! If within ourselves, we are to judge the works of nature as beautiful we must identify them, not necessarily within the conventions of our time and the way that we are told to believe, but as we personally identify ourselves with natural scenes and essences. Our feelings can be instinctive or self-taught. These sensibilities may later deceive us but even so such recognitions serve as a signal in the future. A false signal can vitalize our thinking by transmitting a new point of departure. Even an erroneous feeling of this kind is better than no recognition at all.

Being able to interpret what we actually see and feel about a scene in nature is very much akin to being our own artist. These creative perceptions build an ever widening stream of recognitions and allow us to develop faith in our own judgment, the revelation of our own opinions. Why is it that we so often enjoy nature more in a gallery than in a real life experience? Are we incapable of creating our own artistic illusions? Why are we afraid to face nature directly, to interpret her moods, to make them work for us, to see new potentials in old relations? Do we subconsciously recognize our precarious condition on earth or feel our ancestor's struggle for survival in the wild? Is the realism of nature so disagreeable that we can only enjoy the idealizations of the museum? Or, are we fearful of our own values, our own beliefs? Have we become so docile, biddable and directed that we can only enjoy what we are told is good?

Since biblical Genesis our fear of water has only been exceeded by our need for it. The hydrologic cycle: evaporation, clouds, rain, drainage to the sea, and back again is the source of life on earth. Water covers three-fourths of the face of the globe and is the single greatest agent for transformation that we know. Water represents the ultimate metamorphosis, both in its own kind and in its effects upon others. It is no accident that in Greek mythology, Poseidon, god of the sea, also created earthquakes; a god of destruction and a god of plenty!

Water may serve as a prefix to more expressions than any other word in the English language. Water tortures of the orient and water ordeals of Europe use water as an ultimate threat of punishment; whether a drop at a time on an exposed head, plunging a bare arm into boiling water as a test for truthfulness, or keel-hauling to extract truth. Water is deeply engrained in our most ancient mythology and was recognized even in pre-scientific chemistry as one of the four or five elements from which all else was made. Water has long and simultaneously related sublime beauty and ultimate horror.

When these photographs of water were taken years ago, I was not considering labels such as moody and happy. However, one group of pictures seems to lift my spirits while the other, more powerful in some ways, leaves me more morose or downcast. The happy group gives me greater pleasure, satisfaction, and a conscious sense of well being, while the moody group tends to depress and create a subtle sense of discontent. Anger and foreboding in one group contrast starkly with the effervescent sense of joy in the other. Such elusive and emotional responses are not easily explained but must involve such generalized factors as movement, horizon, tactility, light, clarity, color, and a sense of the importance of space. Each of these forces is associated with all of the others in my mind, and it is here and not on the surface of the retina that final judgments are made. The ultimate appraisal begins with our senses but it always culminates with the nurturing of ideas within the brain.

The sense of touch or tactility, is probably the most acute of our senses and is related to each of the photographs that follow. The sense of touch relates to fear and love; to brutal blows and soft caresses. Tactile gratification can give joy and enhance life but touch can also cause flesh to crawl and goose bumps to rise. Almost all strong visual experiences have a tactile element, an exposure so vital as to produce a sense of touching, whether seemingly actual or purely psychological. With water the emotion can range from a feeling of spray on the face to total immersion and lack of balance; from joyous water play to turbulent drowning. Such visual and tactile concatenations underlie my judgment of each of the following photographs, whether happy or moody.

Space, with its edges or horizon is also evident in our responses to photographs, but perhaps not as intensely as movement. We have come to find that the space between objects is often as important to our satisfaction as the objects themselves. While we have always known that this was the case with music, sculpture, and buildings it was not sometimes recognized elsewhere. In some instances such as in living spaces, the objects really exist only to define the space in between. Throughout the ancient world the space between structures was often as important as the structures themselves. Examples include the pyramids at Gizeh,

precolumbian ruins from Peru to Mexico, and the spaces between buildings on the Acropolis in Athens. The flow of the space about objects and the object's relation to the horizon, all affect our interpretation of what we see. Space joins with motion to create very elaborate and complex responses in the viewer.

The processes that alter earlier mental images often anticipate a new perception and so prepares our minds to receive new information. This knowlege may not coincide with what the retina, alone, transfers to the brain. Mental images of this kind can enhance or prejudice a perception by improperly stimulating neural mechanisms within the visual system. Earlier interpretations of visual phenomena can stimulate neural events equal to those occurring at the moment that something is first seen. The perceptual process is greatly altered by these preexisting mental images that in less scientific terms can simply be called earlier experiences.

Each of us create our own peculiar mental images regarding specific types of objects, scenes, and actions. The holistic image that we develop depends upon the knowledge that we accumulate and this includes such factors as content, size, shape, color, and movement. Once developed these visceral images take on a life that is almost their own. They are, for all practical purposes, autonomous. These preexisting mental images acquire powers within the mind that alter perception itself.

Movement, particularly with an encompassing vehicle such as water, develops mental images within all of us. Our minds can interpret minute differences in the movement of water whether slow and sullen, limpid and placid, highly transparent or darkly ominous. Water can swirl, fall, rush, jump, and riffle as it alters its movement and our interpretations. As movements change, our underlying mental images return to earlier perceptions as reflected in our descriptions of inanimate things: rivers run, grass waves, and fogs cling.

Like movement, size, particularly as it relates to the human body and the position of the horizon, reveals the viewer's location and relationship, and interacts with earlier experiences to create mental images that alter our direct visual interpretation of what we see. Safety and the relative running speed of humans and carnivores are probably related to the maximum length of today's shopping malls and our sense of well being when walking on a darkened street. Everything that we see has recollective tenacles in the remote past.

The attributes of each of nine photographs will be discussed as they hold qualitative significance for me. Each was selected as representing something satisfying, whether based upon visual images accreted from the past or simply striking a chord of unexplained response.

In *Photo 22, Leaking Earth, Iguacu, Brazil, 1977*, the verdure of subtropical vegetation is entwined with layers of dripping or rushing cataracts. Life sustaining water is coupled with a sense of its destructive power as it rushes toward the unknown, transmuting itself from cloud, to rain, to mist, to animal and vegetable life, and back again to its beginning. The pure joy of raw existence is given symbol by both the onrush of the water and the almost impertinent upthrust of the resisting stone with a palm tree clinging to its crest.

The Iguacu cataracts are over two and a half miles wide and shaped in a great crescent. They combine the discomfort of both extreme heat and humidity. No photograph can convey their steamy roar. Once called "Victoria Falls," like those on the Zambezi River, over twenty cataracts average more than two hundred feet in height.

In comparison *Photo 23, Cascadas Agua Azul, near Ocosingo, Chiapas, Mexico, 1984*, are rapids rather than cataracts even though both produce playful white water. Here, the water rushes over six or eight steps of vertical exuberance. The movement, while much less grandiose than at Iguacu, is actually more moving to the human psyche because of its more intimate scale. Without a visible horizon the water seems to appear from nowhere as it takes its joyous and tactile trip downward to the viewer. There is a sense of touch here, as though you were sitting on a stairstep and can actually feel the water sweep over you.

Photo 24, Lake Chapala, Jalisco, Mexico, 1991, records a calm dusk on an inland lake. The tangle of boats in the foreground competes for attention with the eternal mountains in the distance, but the whole scene is dominated by translucent light and moving clouds. The intimate grandeur of nature and its association of ageless mountains and water is contrasted with the transience of man. A sense of expansive well being is not denied by the ominous clouds and foreboding night. These images will remain in the mind, both as derivatives of the past and predicates of the future. Tranquility and peace permeate the air as they mix with earlier images of the imagined and the remembered.

Water can also scintillate with flashing power and sensual delight. *Photo 25, Spring Waterfall, Flam to Gol, Norway, 1986*, shows a Scandinavian watergap that is giddy and vertiginous as it noisily splashes its way from the snows above. The view places the viewer in the midst of pure merriment and the awesome beauty of a seasonal moment. With a zestful tumbling that would overpower any amusement park ride, the photograph requires the viewer to recollect moments of complete abandon, times to feel, to live to the fullest.

Such wild exuberance cannot last but must be appreciated for the moment. Like the wild abandon of youth, the effrontery of a puerile fighter pilot in wartime, the jaunty spring watergap will pass on to the growing maturity of a more lasting tranquility.

Photo 26, Island Cave Near Tortola, British West Indies, 1976, illustrates a greater sense of calm and the acceptance of a more gentle passage of time. Here, on small islands, such as Virgin Gorda, mountains, sea, and coral interact to create brilliant color combinations. Like reflected jewels the seawater becomes limpid and lustrous as it mixes with coral and the romantic potential of a beckoning cave. Who can react to this photograph without a romantic thought of buccaneers and their small boats loaded with booty? Limited in scope but exuding such images this scene demands sensuous swim of exploration and tactile response. The only horizon is seen as the mirrorlike reflection of a cave mouth on the shadowed wall.

Photo 27, Sea of Crete, South of Athens, Greece, 1980, shows by ominous contrast the foamy froth of a ship's wake as a storm cloud approaches and promises neither calm nor security. The light variations, while compositionally exciting, do not portend happy sailing. The scene is menacing, even frightening. The shapes and colors are much like those associated with a waterspout with its rapidly rotating, cloud-filled wind. We can sense the spray torn by the whirling winds. A torrent is building in the sky with depression and a mood of ill-temper. Gloom and fearful expectation fills the air and terror is balanced against a sense of growing excitement. We can almost feel the movement of the clouds, the wind, the water, and its currents, even the anticipation of pressure changes. Looking becomes feeling. We have passed from the happy expectation of sunlight to a demonstration of raw strength. Our mind is working. We are relating what we see and sense to what we have felt under similar conditions in the past. We are exploring a new experience, with moodiness perhaps, but also with a sense of new potentials. The mysteries within our minds are closely tied to our feelings at such times. Our complete visual potential is at work.

Trepidation and nervous agitation can be as much a matter of the theatrics of accidental light as of real danger. *Photo 28, Mae Kok River, Thailand-Burma Border, 1987*, captures a moment, a mood of fear, caused by an accidental combination of the visual effects of color, light, and cloud formation. Actually, the moment was indeed one of concern; armed guards were riding "shotgun" in our boat near the infamous "golden triangle" between Burma and Thailand. The photograph has nothing to do with this real concern but does create a foreboding impression, a seeming dark and dangerous moment. Cloudy, silt-filled water connotes impurity, dangerous opacity, and uncleanness. When compounded by approaching storm clouds and the visual effect of a current flowing over a submerged obstacle to create an ominous whirlpool, a mood of enveloping concern grew.

Photo 29, Inle Lake near Taunggyi, Burma, 1987, is really a happy and expectant view of a lake dweller's remote village in the midst of exotic floating gardens. Located miles from solid ground, all services are water borne. Except for the strangeness of the surroundings and the turbid, roily lake's surface the scene has an interesting vitality; however, the perverse brown color of the water taints the scene. A distant horizon and the summer clouds cannot dispel the oppressiveness created by the dismal water's surface. Something dank and contaminated outweighs the attraction of the quaint trading village. Perhaps the source of my unease originated in recollections of a swollen and flooding Mississippi River, the indistinct mental image that things are not quite right and could get worse.

Fast moving rivers are cantankerous. Even when their rapids are only riffles they can give the impression of impending wrath; their disposition is full of discontent and they are tempermental. This melancholia is evident in the Hunza River as it rushes to meet the great Indus. It is said that the Indus River roars from the jaws of a mythical lion, as it drops twelve thousand feet to meet the Arabian Sea four hundred miles away. Along the way, the valleys that it trespasses are composed of fine, pale sands of pink and tarnished gray, with patches here and there of the greens and yellows of laborious irrigation. The Karakoram mountain range, with a majority of the highest mountain peaks in the world over twenty thousand feet in height, seems to be composed of soft, loose, and shifting rocks, gravel, and sand. Drivers look alongside the rutted roads for sliding boulders rather than ahead for other vehicles. *Photo 30, Hunza River near Khunjerab Pass, Karakoram Mountains, Pakistan, 1989,* depicts a dramatic, dangerous, and moody mountain environment. The mood swings of the river itself are pronounced and physically felt by the observer. With spring thaws the waters sweep forward carrying vast accumulations of silt and boulders and cleaning the valleys of all before them. Here, a suspension bridge defiantly faces the inevitable onslaught of the river. The rocky remains of last year's excesses are overlooked by the mass of sliding erosion that will oppose the river's currents for years to come. A world of transience, movement, change, and instability gives the feeling that an irresistible force is softly threatening an immovable object. Irrevocable change, alongside determined resistance, is everywhere. Rainclouds surround the truculent peaks. Here, miles above an accepting sea, only occasional rays of sunlight pierce slits in cloud bottoms to relieve the oppression. Without human habitation and vegetation the only trace of life is the erosion of washed-out roads and terraces. This scene has been added to previous visual images where God seems to allow little hope for the future. The scene produces a sense of deep melancholy but strangely, at the same time, is uplifting, hopeful. The outlook is at the same moment both calm and restive; a place to begin renewal of the human spirit; a purgatory that promises hopeful beginnings.

From the Iguacu to the Hunza happiness and moodiness converge and then reverse themselves, neither more powerful in our thoughts than the other, but both significant for what they can portend. Both happy water and moody water are components of a vital life; and while mood may be no more than a consciously subjective state of mind, happiness is much more than our calm accommodation to what is. In our responses and satisfactions there can be no majestically final truths. There is only a growing appreciation of nature, ourselves within it, and the determination to learn from what we see.

VI SEASHORES—SUNRISES AND SUNSETS

Seashores and the daily arrival and departure of the sun create emotional responses within all of us. Why is this so? Could our feelings rest in our unknown past and have been handed down to us through our parents? Will we pass this inheritance along to our children while adding our own individual sensitivities to the accumulations of the past? Or is our love of the seashore founded in the dim obscurity of a previous existence when, as Loren Eiseley explains in *The Immense Journey*, we came wiggling out of the sea on our fins? Does our infatuation with sunrises and sunsets rest at the beginning of creation when the giver of all life on earth first poked itself above the horizon? Are these daily momenets descended from the same sensations of touch described by the fingers of Michelangelo's figures on the ceiling of the Sistine Chapel?

Seashores and the sun's coming and going are nature's symbols of a deep personal resonance recognized throughout the world. They represent elemental opposites; life and death, day and night, beginning and end; they are religiously and psychologically significant, and they have an unequivocal universality. I believe that such signatures of belief are carried from generation to generation. They are not learned. They are just there!

As I considered these thoughts I heard the lilting song of a mockingbird. How had it learned those captivating sounds; who was its teacher? And why are mocking birds, hundreds of miles apart, singing the same identical tunes? It is certainly not mocking. Is it telepathy, the result of genetics, or what? Could our human responses to some recurring natural events, whether in Nepal or Louisiana, be related in the same way? Do bird's songs and certain human reactions have similar instinctive sources? I believe that they do. It has been shown that a young bird held in auditory isolation, and without contact with its kind, will experiment with sound when it is a few weeks old. Later, the song of the specie is slowly developed and adapted and, except for minor variations, maintained, whether the bird is kept in isolation or released to mix with its own kind.

As birds, bees, and rats have been shown to be guided by forces inherent in their genetic makeup, so are people. I believe that many of our tendencies, abilities, and preferences are controlled by little understood instinctual forces; otherwise, why aren't we nocturnal, and why do we seek the rewards that we do? Answers to such questions could give us a better understanding of why we are drawn by the visual challenge of the seashore and why we sit in rapt wonder before the sun when it is near the horizon.

I am not privy to the wonders of psychology, but I have found that an apparent specialty within the trade has adopted the term "ethnology" for the study of the formation of human character, animal behavior, and instinct. Their views differ from those of psychological behaviorists who seem to limit their concerns to learning under controlled conditions, disregarding the forces of heredity. These differences in approach become important when using their study results to guide our thinking as to why we like or dislike certain scenes or photographs.

The behaviorists divide their conditions of animal learning into two groups that they refer to as classical or operant conditioning. Under classical conditioning, we automatically react to cues, the way that Pavlov's dogs salivated when they heard the dinner bell, regardless of whether food followed or not. Under operant conditioning, behavior patterns are learned from trial-and-error, as with rats in a maze, where patterns of behavior are observable and measurable.

The ethnologists, on the other hand, with their concerns for genetic transpositioning, have used four factors to gauge animal behavior that seems to me to apply equally to humans. These include: *instinctive recognition of symbols, innate physical responses, conditions and timing of motivations*, and the *capacity for specialized understanding or insights*.

As we look, as we are conditioned by what we see and the way in which we interpret the scenes shown in a photograph, we know that our past experiences, that our limited life styles with their acquired lessons, can never explain the entire range of our sensibilities. Something tells us that we are more understanding and more at home in some places, in some environments, than in others. I believe that I am preprogrammed to respond to specific inherited symbols in quite precise ways. My reaction to impersonal photographs tells me that instinct, learning, and appreciation are mutually reinforcing, that I could not be the same if my parents had married other partners, if my genes were different. The accident of my parents joining, for better or for worse, has made me as I am. I am, and I see, through their eyes and the eyes of their forebearers, not in exactly the same way but with many profound similarities. But, then again, I am just partly like either of my parents, for better or for worse.

To make these thoughts clearer I would like to relate my appreciation of three photographs of seashores to the four factors used by ethnologists to measure animal behavior. The photographs include: *Photo 31, Island of Mykonos, Greece, 1980; Photo 32, Seaside Between Cape Point and Capetown, Republic of South Africa, 1981*; and *Photo 33, Tulum Ruins, Yucatan, Mexico, 1988.*

The instinctive recognition of symbols is probably the strongest force underlying our reaction to a visual scene. The proportion of learned to inherited values is not known, but I believe that most simple responses have deep instinctive roots lying below their environmental, associative, and learned relations. For instance, a sense of exposure and the effects resulting from the abrasive edge of land, as it confronts the sea, must pass from generation to generation. These conditions are evident in all three photographs but are more pronounced in *Photos 32 and 33*. We can see and feel erosion at work in *Photo 32*; the abrasive action of the rocky shore is emphasized by the foam, eddies, and turbulence of the water. The confrontation of stone, ocean currents, tides, and winds is engraved upon the surfaces of the shoreline and within the mind's core of genetic experience.

In all of these scenes we sense the exposure of man to the elements, the seafarer in his milieu, the opposing forces of land and water. Such instructive symbols are complex, but they are latent with feelings for all of us. In *Photos 31 and 33*, we sense docile bodies of water but realize that their apparent calm can be a caprice. The very reason that we find seashores so attractive may be their deceptiveness. *Photo 31* gives token of a safe harbor, where religion, commerce, industry and recreational beauty are combined. The symbolic contrast of cutting barnacles, with their mucoid slime, and the neat white church relates faith, reality, and the risks of life with Poseidon. *Photo 33* intimates greater physical safety, between sea and land, but while the sea is more tractable, man's forces against it are more rigid and less sympathetic than the Aegean shoreline. In *Photo 32*, visual symbols include turbulence, restive aggression, and an incessant assault upon the status quo. Such generalized ciphers, while never fully supporting conscious determinations, lie as remembered bedrock in the support of both our imagination and our intuition.

Innate physical responses accompany these instinctive symbols. The vast underpinnings of nature always alter our consciousness. In *Photo 31*, I can feel the slickness alongside the cutting edges of the barnacle-clad stone. The buildings so near the waterline constitute an act of faith. In *Photo 32*, the viewer responds to the lack of footholds on the harsh shore. Dangerous currents, eddies, and undertows are apparent, while more tranquil qualities radiate from *Photo 33*. Here, a sea barrier overlooks seductive white beaches and crystal clear water. The water along with the cool winds running before the rainstorm are literally felt. Such physical responses, collected through the millenia, must lie buried in our genes; for while experience is a great teacher, such wide-ranging perceptions go beyond any learned familiarity.

Conditions and timing of motivation alter our learned responses. How else can we explain man's universal search for sweeping panoramic views and high places? Prominent visual vantage points are a part of mankind's perennial search. In *Photo 31*, we sense soft, midday summer breezes along with a calm horizon, while in *Photo 33*, the sweeping panorama of sea and distant shore affirm the pleasures of sunrise, worship, and the afternoon shade. Only *Photo 32* reveals nature's incessant opposition, prevailing winds, and changing tides. Here, in a winter without snow, the terrible energy of nature's forces charge the scene.

The *capacity for specialized understanding of insights* is difficult to separate from habit and heredity. The builders of the structures shown in *Photos 31 and 33* consulted wind, waves, topography, and religious beliefs and then decided upon their sacred places. Each, in a sensitive way, combines a building site with the imaginative instincts of their forebearers. The shadows of past ideas and intuitions are here incorporated into the conscious knowledge of their own time. *Photo 32* represents an ultimate challenge for someone in our time to create a community as natural and instinctively secure as those shown on Mykonos or at Tulum.

It is apparent to me that all of us are affected by the environment that we know, often through the conditioning of our ancestors. This instructive response that is passed down to us is much more than a proclivity to salivate when called upon, or to learn from the obvious rewards of trial and error. Instinctual conditioning is not so much whether we choose to understand as it is whether we are capable of understanding; not whether we are a battery ready to receive a quantity of electrical charge, but whether we are capable of receiving the proper voltage.

There are uplifting visual events in each of our lives when our minds rise above immediate necessities and worldly cares. We can be visually overpowered for a moment, and it is at times like these that our core values are most likely to change. I am convinced that our ability to learn, to alter our values permanently, occurs at moments of great tranquility, beauty, and joy, and that these moments respond to inherited values.

Who can look at *Photo 34, Sunrise, Danube River, Budapest, Hungary, 1984,* and not sense the welcome of the coming day? There is no need to dissect the scene, the river mist overriding and obscuring the symbolic seat of government, the spires rising to honor God, the impertinent little group of leaves sharing the centerstage with man's most powerful institutions. At this calm moment the ideology of the place is a backdrop for creative thought.

A contrary condition, *Photo 35, Sunset, Meteora Monastery, Kalambaka, Greece, 1990,* has its incised silhouette emphasized by the drab and cloudy sky beyond the rocky profile. The sun pierces the scene to direct the eye to the monastery's solitary remoteness. The clouds serve as a cyclorama to give visual dominance to the remote building as the setting sun reverses conditions shown in *Photo 34.* The scene is primordial. Twenty-five thousand years ago it must have been human responses to such scenes as this that allowed humanity to explode with symbolic creations. The instincts of primitive man, when he began his search for the reason for life, required high and defensible places such as seen here. Certainly such scenes are imbedded in our collective psyche and must be partially responsible for directing our growing beliefs through their suggestive presence.

The same colors and tonal values bring together ideological settings in Greece and in *Photo 36, Sunset, Baguio, Luzon, Philippines, 1987.* Along a mountain ridge trees thrust skyward as if preparing for the coming darkness. Their isolated profiles demand individual attention; the viewer cannot escape the temerity of their precarious existence, nor the parallels between their struggles for life and our own. Such symbolic

transfers between plant and human are felt throughout our mythology and animal inheritance. Why else are our spirits so lifted by failing sunlight and clinging trees?

Sunrise or sunset, the edge of things, the horizon, plays a dominant visual role. We look to our world's edge to reassure ourselves that it is still there. Where would we be without the horizon to position us on earth? Any aviator, prisoner or agoraphobic understands. To most of us distance is reassuring, but the fear of open space or height can also be appalling and must be another example of a perhensile instinct. Throughout the ages, the horizon, coupled with water overviews, has had mystical connotations. *Photo 37, Sunrise, Ganges River, Varanasi, India, 1985,* is an example of this. Here, "the river of enlightenment," the Ganges, slowly winds its way past the bathing steps and smoking cremation ghats. As the sun rises, thousands of Hindus of all ages and ranks share the muddy water with bloated human corpses and water buffalo. These insanitary conditions disgust the western viewer who has vastly different values. Hinduism does not require adherence to a single religious dogma or demand specific devotion to its many gods. For Hindus, the Ganges is a mythical river of hope and salvation and they hold it in absolute reverence, even beyond personal health. As the sun rises over the Ganges, ritual bathers' eyes record the significance of the moment. They stand transformed by a spirit that extends beyond worldly substance. As work boats carrying wood to the cremation platforms glide by and black water buffalo snort in the shallow water, the bathers on the bank are oblivious to everything but the glowing sun as it transforms the scene and spreads to the farthest horizon. Anther day has begun and man's ideologic mission on earth revives itself. Even the most doubting visitor is struck by such acts of faith, particularly when they are so dramatically coupled with the earth's daily renewal.

At moments like this, nature's dependable scheme of systematic reiteration is imbedded in our individual ideologies. The fundamental values that permeate our every act are taking shape. Our ethos is molded by such visual experiences. A millenium and a half ago St. John Chrysostom wrote: "Who does not despise all the creations of art, when at dawn in the stillness of his heart he admires the rising sun as it sheds its golden light over the earth."

Does it surprise anyone that with civilization's relentless urban concentration and man's steady retreat from intimate associations with land, plants, and nature, that we find fewer rewards and satisfactions? Less than two percent of the population of the United States now produces all of our foodstuffs. While agricultural activities still dominate our rural landscapes the power of agrarian values of the past is gone. Today, the farm and the farmer are widely considered anachronistic.

VII   FIELDS AND MEADOWS

Looking backward to my review of a group of ideographic photographs, I find that the general subject of fields and meadows has long been very important to me. Apparently my rural upbringing and the traditions of my immediate forebearers influenced this pastoral side of my nature. Or perhaps, as another restless and incensed city dweller, I realize that a greater potential for life and personal expression is missing in cities but must exist in rural environments. In any event, nostalgia was involved in the selection of the nine scenes shown here. As a group, they seem to oppose urban concentrations and man's seeming predisposition to assemble into groups and, like sheep, to always seek collective advantage and termite-like living conditions.

It is an irony indeed that the pastoral scenes shown here only apply to earlier definitions of the word, as it pertained to animal shepherds and country life. I am deeply opposed to the current use of the word as it refers to the spiritual care and guidance of a flock of human souls. I resist the idea that another fallible human being should assume responsibility for the adequacy of my innermost faith and beliefs. Is it not strange that the title given to a herder of one of the world's most mentally limited animals should come to occupy a position of such profound religious importance? Are we so much like sheep that we will accept such arrogant dullards?

My resentment may have originated during World War II, on the island of Okinawa, when for long periods we were forced to eat either "lamb, ram, or mutton." Did the deep aversion that I developed to the taste and odor of the animal's flesh influence my interpretation of religious guidance? In any event, my use of the word pastoral is here intended to express the simple, rural, open-air life; the land and natural charm associated with nature's open areas. It has no religious connotations whatsoever.

The direct relations of nature and religion, as historically represented by rustic landscapes, melancholy music, and florid literature seems to have reached its zenith in the eighteenth and early nineteenth centuries. The cult of industrialization with its urban agglomerations was just taking hold. Country people lost their reputation for righteousness and social perfection, even as Charles Dickens' sentimental characters introduced the growing problems of urban congestion, pollution, and human degradation to the world. Today, *country* seems to be in the complete thrall of *city*.

Rural and urban have evolved as savage adversaries in more than economic and ethnic conflict. Their values are quite different, and the characteristics of the people are so opposed as to seem irreconcilable. The "rurban" fringe, used since 1918 to describe the borders separating country from town, are no longer recognizable. The contrasts are fixed and comparisons are only valid for supporting media polemics. The two ideologies, the two environments, are in conflict.

Photo 38, Fields and Meadows, Heilbronn, Germany, 1984, represents the well groomed baronial landscape of farms and meadows lying at the edge of a medieval village. Feudal power looks out upon verdant fields and woodlands of manicured stability. It is a Germanic scene of peace and plenty where individual initiatives and energies have culminated in serene predictability. *Photo 39, Sheep on Mountain Meadow, Gulmarg, India, 1985*, displays a flock of sheep grazing on a spring meadow in the Himalayas. Photographed from near a cemetery holding the recently desecrated graves of Bengal Lancers, this old English hill station is more reminiscent of Switzerland or Scotland than of the India that we have read about. Thin mountain soil demands the continuation of the nomadic ways of the sheep herder, for here nature is only transiently kind. *Photo 40, Barley Fields, near Lhasa, Tibet, 1988*, located higher in the Himalayas, appears less luxuriant but has a more productive soil due to its location in a valley near the bank of a stream. The thicker alkaline soil of the arid location is tilled by farmers living in compact villages in the middle of their workplaces. Greatly different, the atmosphere of *Photo 41, Rape Field, Kalmar to Stockholm, Sweden, 1986*, has the intense color combinations of summer lowlands with their richer humus soil. The family farm, a major source of Scandinavian independence, shows the result of generations of care. The independent family unit is supreme. Self sufficiency is possible in such mellifluous natural conditions. Different natural forces are at work in *Photo 42, Flooded Rice Fields, near Rangoon, Burma, 1987*, with a uniform water surface shown stretching to the indistinct horizon. The only relief from water, water, water is the cheniers alongside the river. Here, nature demands the sharing of higher ground and the tillers of the rice paddies live in compact and moldy villages. *Photo 43, Fjord Homestead, Oslo to Balestrom, Norway, 1986*, is located on another kind of water frontage in a different clime. Family groupings displace all but a few villages, and a sense of the open sea, with its brisk winds and erratic changes, replaces the permeating heat and humidity of Burma's marshy rice fields. The individual decision replaces a collective acceptance of the inevitable. Social development and temperature are apparently related. Returning to a warm climate, *Photo 44, Hillside Pasture, San Miguel de Allende, Mexico, 1989*, shows a landscape of erosion, denudation, and a wearing-down of the alkalitropic hillsides into ragged ravines. Erratic, often excessive rainfall creates a crater-like landscape of desolation that lends its own captivating power and beauty; whereas *Photo 45, Scandinavia Mosaic, near Stockholm, Sweden, 1986*, records a distinctly different kind of moist, spring beauty. The tapestry of rich farmlands is verdant as fields and plants luxuriate in fertile soil. This rich and sublime time of growth is starkly different to *Photo 46, Farm Terraces, near Paro, Bhutan, 1989*. Farmers on these parched hillsides eke out a survival subsistence. The intemperate locations oppose nature as steep mountain slopes are forced to accommodate an ill-fitting agriculture.

The contrast between *Photo 38* and *Photo 46* emphasizes several basic dissimilarities. A careful comparison would show many differences, but in a larger view—concerning the most important aspects of what I see in these two photographs—how do I interpret what is most significant to me? Is it geographic location, general environment, weather, government, or mere color? The scope of choices has narrowed, but a great number always remain. Can my ultimate decision be swayed by the vagaries of pictorial composition, knowing one way of life better than the other, or some even more remote and subjective thought that I cannot even bring into focus? I do not really know the answer, but in the instant of appraisal I am much more attracted to the Bhutan mountainside than to the rich green German landscape. Perhaps it is the unknown aspects of a strange culture or the desire to participate in needed change. However, somewhere buried within my past, my genes, my schooling, or my experience I am more rewarded by what I see in Bhutan than in Germany. Even this brief and superficial analysis gives me more confidence for the way in which I arrive at my value judgments, even though I realize that my methods may change at any moment.

Space will not permit the contrast of each picture with the other eight; however, I feel quite certain, for example, that contrasting *Photo 41* and *Photo 46* would produce about the same reactions as those just described. The contrast between *Photo 39* and *Photo 45* balances the greens of a herdsman overseeing his mountainside flock and the tapestry of rich lowland fields and meadows. One consists of almost iridescent colors and emphasizes the transient moment, while the other is timeless; yet I find them equally satisfying.

In *Photo 40* and *Photo 42*, the village located in the irrigated barley field, in Tibet, is compared to the watery world of Burma's summer rice paddies. One shows the subtle colors of the high plateau, while the other reflects only monochromatic water and mist. One infers the free choice of association, while the other commands its people to group for survival. Great beauty is placed alongside utter necessity. Both overcome the adversities of nature and geographic location, but somehow one connotes more choices than the other. In one, I might meet the sunrise with expectation, while in the other I could only hope for changes in the season. In the Burma scene I can sense the sticky mud between by calloused toes and feel trapped within a moribund horizon. In the Tibetan view, the profiles of clouds and mountain ridges are a source of constant emotional support. One scene is vital, if impoverished; the other while probably much richer in worldly terms, foretells only gloom, bruising labor, and musty forebearance. One seems healthy and whole, while the other reminds me of mosquitoes and mold.

Photo 43, the Norwegian fjord, and *Photo 44*, the eroded hillside in Mexico, are in many respects the opposites of one another, an ultimate contrast. Yet, to choose between them to say which most satisfies my inner being, which gives my conscious mind, my aesthetic being, the greater gratification; which contains the magic of a returning eye; which nearer satisfies my ideals, and approaches my chosen ethos; is difficult, for it does not make economic or logical sense to make such a choice. One is lush and verdant; the other dry, eroded, and deformed. How can I account for such visual perversion if I choose the Pyrrhic victory of an arid and deprived locale to one of temperate ease? Sensing a certain rape of logic, I wonder why the Mexican photograph gives me a sense of freedom, even with its stunted and sun-cooked plants, emaciated cattle, and dust enfolded barrenness? Is it contrariness, something within my inheritance, or does adversity and the will to overcome it, have its own special appeal? *Photo 44* has a taunting reality, while *Photo 43* is already part of an exotic heaven on earth. One represents strife and the potential for needed change; the other was merely born rich.

Reviewing these nine photographs of fields and meadows alongside my comparison, contrasts, and ultimate choices I realize that at the last moment all of my final decisions were based upon subjective and seemingly fallacious reasoning. Try as I will, my objective analysis almost always fails at the last moment, and subjective forces take command. Yet I know that these efforts to understand my preferences will alter what I feel in the future. Perhaps astronomers are right, space is curved, and we can only see truth a short distance ahead. With this contortion of reason I will now consider nature's mystification and illusions. Unlike mathematicians I do not feel responsible for creating order from chaos. I may actually prefer a little chaotic abandon. Unity, infinity, harmony, proportion, balance, and clarity are often beyond my conceptual control, for when I sum up all such factors I often prefer something else.

VIII   NATURE CONCEALS AND ILLUSION

We are all perplexed and bewildered by nature and its overpowering domination of our existence. Nature establishes the essential constitution, construction, and operation of everything. It includes the entire material world along with its creative and regulatory powers. Nature is unchangeable in its laws but ever changing in it attributes. The ultimate mysteries of life are compounded within nature and apparently nothing is unnatural except that concocted within the human mind. As our eyes record nature we observe a pattern of repetitive cycles and perpetual change. Only images and memories remain static. Nature is forever altering material things; water evaporates, plants die, seasons change, and animals evolve and then disappear.

My definition of nature includes all worldly changes beyond the control of man; the way the earth would be whether all animal life existed or not, the character and constitution of everything in its ultimate condition. Nature, as I use the word, cannot be good or bad, for it is the cause of all phenomena. We can extract some constituents from nature and temporarily reform them to our needs, but we can never alter the essentials. Nature reforms and readapts all of man's efforts.

The forces of nature often seem ambiguous. The cumulus cloud calmly floats by, majestic against the cerulean blue of the sky. Its benevolent shade and cooling breezes do not reveal the turbulence within.

Whether the exemplar is clouds, the insidious and often dangerous beauty of insects or the measured grace of a stalking cat, nature does not always reveal its true intentions in terms that we understand. Nature obfuscates and disguises, in terms of our past experience. As we recognize such ambiguities our interpretations change and we often salvage advantage from what earlier seemed troublesome impediments. Through the study and proper understanding of natural phenomena, man has drastically improved his condition on earth.

Looking at nature, learning its ways, is a never ending search that is always just beginning. The mechanics of the way that the mind-eye functions confounds us and is beyond my real comprehension, but I would like to convey my current view of this complex phenomenon in very general terms. The description that follows is not intended as an accurate scientific explanation of this complex subject. This construal is only meant to help the reader to seek an enlarging comprehension of the interrelated activities of the eye-brain.

Through the years I have developed a personal explanation of the visual process as I simplisticly conceive its mechanical operation. The system of recognition that I use rests upon two sequential steps. The first involves an almost automatic initial scan. The second step requires an extended focus upon the object or scene under consideration. The first scan is almost completely automatic, but the second is not.

The first instinctive scan may not be instantaneous; however, the routes that the message takes between retina and brain require very little precognition. The second step demands prior experience, judgment, and rational thought. The first act in my assumed theory of visual recognition terminates in a gestalt, an overview of the complete scan, probably a single identifying cerebral symbol. The following act demands that I focus all of my accumulated experience upon a point of fresh awareness where a new beginning is possible.

The first step, symbolic image recognition, consists of repeated incremental flashes of dark and light, usually perceived as a fleeting glance. These accumulated and separately indistinguishable views, many times faster than the blink of an eye, can be thought of as much like looking through both windows of a slowly passing train to see what is located on the other side. These chains of increments build into a whole, a generalization of the entire visual field. This comprehensive image is recorded in the brain for future use through symbols. These image symbols are the basis for future analogic comparisons that immediately follow.

The millisecond sequence of events leading to what we see as an identifiable object or setting, which I refer to here as the first step, can be visualized and drawn as a series of two dimensional hour-glass shapes stacked vertically on top of one another. The bottom triangle-shaped chamber of each hour-glass is about twice the size of the chamber immediately above. In this fashion three or four two-chamber hour-glasses, representing six or eight enlarging triangular shapes, are equivalent to the same number of windows on the passing train. The top of the uppermost hour-glass represents the first fraction of a millisecond of our glance as we recognize only the very general features, light and dark, line and edge. The lines converge to the throat of the hour-glass where the subject is first seen in its entirety and then transmitted to the brain. In the brain it is automatically coordinated, and passed on to the top of the second hour-glass where such added features as color, texture, and brightness are received with an unconscious rapidity and again returned to the brain for automatic encoding and further coordination. The third and later cycles of these fast-as-light transmissions which we perceive as a single distinguishable scene, can include direction, movement, and all the other enlarging components of automatic recognition. The bottom of the lowest hour-glass represents a gestalt-whole of the entire scene or visual field and as such is finally recorded in the brain. This single symbolic remembrance of the seen image, as it was accumuluated from the numerous, practically instantaneous cross communications between retina and brain, is recorded alongside those already there and others to be obtained later, and then called upon for comparsion and use. It should be noted that the bases of the downward enlarging hour-glasses represent the mechanical accumulation of new data, while the throat of each hour-glass characterizes a partial, but growing synthesis.

These spontaneous and involuntary recognitions are constantly challenged by nature's concealments. Interpreting nature's obvious disguises requires that the process be tested to its ultimate. What is meant by disguise, concealment, obscurity? Nature is not deceptive and does not deal in artifice. When we fail to comprehend nature's intentions it is our own incapacity, not a dissembling nature, that misleads us. This apparent concealment is often based upon unusual associations, placements, and combinations. There is great satisfaction to be enjoyed when a deeper understanding of such camouflage becomes clear.

The very fact that nature does not stroll naked across the earthly stage adds to its interest and inscrutability. Obscurity contributes mystique, even to nature, allowing a feeling of greater satisfaction when we come to understand something in a new way. Such impressions can produce an enlarged, or reduced, reality, for we often attribute our responses to what does not exist, or have no response to what does. This misinterpretation of the nature of something creates misleading illusions, often with analogic connotations. William Blake said: "But to the eyes of the man of imagination nature is imagination itself. As a man is, so he sees."

Mystical human responses are associated with many types of concealment and illusion. They reside within our mental recesses and may, in some people, express deep seated spiritual needs. They are based upon intuition, learned superstition, and the occult, and arise from little understood experiences. Mystic responses occur through vicarious associations and are not instant responses to visual perceptions alone. Mysticism often perplexes the viewer of religious symbols as they seek greater religious understanding at the expense of reason.

Visual responses should be recognized and analzyed by the reader as the second step of any appraisal as he seeks to interpret individual photographs. Each scene contains innumerable coded messages that are directly related to nature's tendency for varying its concealments.

Photo 47, Becan Ruins, Yucatan, Mexico, 1988, at first scan is a rocky hillside covered with exotic plants. It is from such soothing reminders of human fate that archaeologists and anthropologists trace our ancestors. Here, nature is not alone in her concealments. This disguised, plant laden Maya pyramid probably conceals a number of manmade constructions within, each built to conceal the other below. At least one probably has funerary remains. Human and natural forces of wind, rain, dust and erosion combine with willing plant growth to create a provocative image of man's vulnerability. The only timeless quality recognizable here is change itself. The mystifying Mayan religious impulse to build thousands of these perplexing and astronomically related centers lends an indefinable enchantment to their superficial exploration by tourists. The spirits of the past join with the needs of the present to create a tourist market of substance. Could this romantic inducement exist without nature's concealment? The most easily known is not always the most desirable.

Photo 48, Great Plaza, Tikal, Guatemala, 1987, shows a portion of one of the world's most remarkable constructions. This classic Maya courtyard, completely surrounded by ceremonial structures and filled with memorial stelae, once accommodated rituals of great splendor. When one climbs to the entrances of the temples facing one another atop Pyramids I and II, visions of the past well-up in the mind. Why was this built? Why was it forgotten? What sort of culture could build and support thousands of such constructions in Mexico, Guatemala, and Honduras? For a fleeting instant these pryamids have been unearthed and temporarily exposed to human view and wonder. How long will this exhumation last? During this moment of geologic time, the spirit of the makers invades the conscience of the visitor. Nature has been momentarily defrocked, and the visitor senses the impatience of the natural tropical growth to again get on with its work. Soon the cloak of concealment will return. It is already beginning at all of the edges and in all of the cracks.

Photo 49, Kruger National Park, Republic of South Africa, 1981, and *Photo 50, Fatehpur Si-Kri, near Agra, India, 1985*, utilize plants to obliterate views of animals and buildings. The camouflage of grazing animals is almost complete. How can the evolutionary process so closely match the colors of skin and grass? Even the darker hair colors are vertical and shaped to emulate the nearby plant stems. A simple count of animals is difficult. The disguise is nearly complete and the specie endure. An equally deceptive act of nature screens Akbar's capitol of the Mogul Empire and its Great Gate of Victory. A heirarchy of twigs, to branches, to trunks, come like rivers to innumerable confluences. From the main trunks they bifurcate and trifurcate, over and over, as their interlacing lines disguise the Great Gate just behind. Only one of the domed shapes atop the gate, domes which guided the designers of India's capital buildings in New Delhi, remains visible. The veiled curtain of this tree reflects the arid climate that was the ultimate cause for the abandonment of the complex. Here concealment also serves as a partial explanation.

Photo 51, Temples, I, II, & III, from IV, Tikal Ruins, Guatemala, 1987, records an enveloping rain forest as it covers the remains of an advanced civilization. Such great cities of stone are ultimately obliterated as nature buries their physical remains. Stephen Vincent Benet's *By the Shores of Babylon* is a narrative describing a boy's reaction as he explores the remains of an overgrown Manhattan Island, years after an atomic holocaust. This imaginative episode could have been triggered by a scene such as that shown in *Photo 51*. Each of us, as we overlook archaeological remains, develop personal interpretations, not only concerning what the civilization may have been like, but, of more significance, their importance to us. The very fact that nature eventually obliterates all human effort makes our ephemeral existence more tolerable. It is reassuring to recognize that we are part of a great and moving cavalcade that includes both nature and humanity.

Photo 52, Roadside Merchant, near Victoria Falls, Rhodesia, 1981, records another evanescent moment when an accident of light and subject matter created a vestigial presence from the past. Here, a remnant of a culture, a way of life that no longer exists, is recorded in needlework and crocheting, while land mines lie buried a few miles away. The irrelevancy of what was, is recorded as a dainty and refined material transparency of the artistic tastes of one culture transiently accepted by another. This soft and seemingly familial scene, reminiscent of an Irish or English countryside, contrasts starkly with its location in the heart of Africa.

Photo 53, Market, Lopburi, Thailand, 1987, is also illusive, a misleading image of scraped pigs' heads. Here, amidst their parts, the butcher has not removed the pig's apparent sense of happy appetite. It is eerie that dead, peeled pigs can appear to be happy, but here they are, still in the midst of a gluttonous, Sybaritic scene, watched over by an alert butcher. The entire episode does not sit calmly in place; or is this attributing existence to something that does not exist, or a nonexistence to something that does? It is an upsetting environment, an apparition, situated as it is between calm crocheted tablecloths on a sunny clothesline and the fantasy of a luminescent and luxuriant reflecting pool. The latter scene, *Photo 54, Water Garden, near Denpasar, Bali, Indonesia, 1987*, is both real and ethereal, a diffusion and an irregular bending-back of images. The crystal clear water refracts, reflects, and magnifies objects above, alongside, and within. Clouds are as real as masonry, and reflections dominate corporeal things. Plants above and below the water intermix with clouds and reflected images to create a fragile reality that combines truth and illusion.

Photo 55, Bridge and Television Tower, Vienna, Austria, 1984, speciously shows a bridge that seems to support a very large television tower. While it does not, the quality of the design of both constructions was so impressive and so much alike that I included the photograph for more detailed study. The allusion to electronic and wheeled communication is inescapable and brings forth the illusion of an actual relationship.

While nature often conceals, it seldom creates really harmful illusions. Hurtful deceptions are the creations of man, either intentionally or through false interpretations. Delusions and misconceptions can be read into nature and called illusion, but they only exist within the human mind. Nature properly understood is never malicious even though it may subject us to frequent surprises.

Most of the issues superficially investigated here have dealt with concealment and illusion as they apply in nature and as symbols of cultural construction. We will now turn our attention to people and animals, largely their individual attributes, attitudes, and responses as seen through eight photographs.

IX   PEOPLE AND ANIMALS

To animate something means to give it life, spirit, and vitality. Only people, and perhaps some higher animals, can be animated; however, we use the term loosely. In viewing reproductions of things we often sense that what we see, even when it contains no living creatures, is still animated by the viewer's life and existence. Cartoons bringing lifelike movement to drawings can be said to be animated, but this is not actually true. Such responses demand a close liaison between the living viewer, and the inanimate lines or objects. This mysterious transference between the living observer and the inanimate image is not easily explained, but it does occur. We must subconsciously believe that our living and sensual animal feelings apply to everything.

As we gauge and weigh the contents of the photographs that follow there are innumerable responses that we do not understand. What we are and what we want to become combine with other forces, many of which we do not recognize. Society, representing the collective beliefs of our kind, usually determines the principles that we find important to life. We call these standards and they represent the relative importance of something based upon its worth to each of us and to society as a whole. Individual and societal values are no more than judgments of relative worth. It is important to realize that both our personal values and the standards of society are exposed when we express our opinions, whether in judging photographs or voting in an election.

Appraising the ethos of a photographic image, the vicarious spirit of a person shown, is in a way a judgment of the values held by the photographic image whether it is really due to the selection of the photographer or accident. A person's ethos characterizes his nature, spirit, group, and epoch. The abstract ethos that we mentally construct when we look at a picture represents the ideals, character, and nature of the person that we believe we see in the reflected image. It is much like theater. We interpret the general mood created by the picture as though it were an actor on a stage. It has been said that the distinguishing characteristics of a person, time, or group; the permeating and essential values that lie between passion and caution, constitute its ethos. The same thought, bent in another direction states that a person's character is actuated by personal values, or ethos, and this can be visually detected. As we contemplate the human influences upon a person in a photograph, or the physical things that they surround themselves with, we appraise the values that we detect. Where feelings of pity or melancholy impinge upon this characterization, we refer to this sense of empathetic suffering as pathos, rather than ethos. This projection of subjective feelings seems to infuse the image that we see, and we come to feel that we occupy the skin of the person seen.

People, the creators of their environments, can only be judged within their time and culture, and they are often considered as a unitary whole. Today, as the twentieth century nears its end, the people of the United States have ignored many of the incomparable opportunities that followed victory in World War II. Through sheer luck, location, and timing our society has dominated world affairs for over forty years; however, the hedonistic equalities that we try to force upon other cultures, our blind acceptance of half-hidden but omnipotent religious lobbies, our autocratic market economy that equates ethics and profit, and a culture that so disproportionately rewards enlarging appetites, muscles, net worths, and wasteful leisure cannot long survive. The good and the honorable middle classes of our country have been euchred and used. They cannot continue to carry the entire load of such wasteful misconceptions. "He's not heavy he's my brother," is a warm and touching thought, but such distorted sentiments will not let us continue to win the competition between great nations. Such thoughts are sweet and touching lies. Stretched-out and insecure as our nation now is, between the economics of an ultimate materialism and the shifty benovelence of a "chicken in every pot," the great issue facing the United States is the long-term pursuit of more realistic goals.

Hoping to find a less biased way to analyze our reactions to images of people and animals, the eight photographs that follow are located in distant Asia and Africa. Seven are Buddhist societies, where human values and aspirations are different to those held in Europe and in this country. Perhaps the differences in values and the distance will let us better examine our own prejudices. The comparison between a Christian, urban society of occidental cities and a Buddhist, rural society of oriental villages should allow us to enter their ethos, values, and minds to obtain a different, and perhaps more valid, point of view for ourselves. Without being within the skin of another individual how are we to judge how and what he sees? Do photographs look both ways? I often wonder how the photographee is judging me! Life is not so much remembered by days and years as by such fleeting insights. I find that a brief glance at a photograph that occurred decades ago, such as the warped and ironical smile of General Eisenhower upon hearing that President Truman had removed General Douglas MacArthur from command, can last longer and produce stronger feelings than actually meeting General Eisenhower years later.

Western travelers in the Far East are usually struck by the kindness and civility of the people they meet there. Some of this attitude may be attributed to false subservience because of our greater wealth and technological advances, but it is interesting to note that these people treat their peers much as they treat the visitor. They are considerate, usually take time for ritual courtesies, and are apparently less hedonistic. Their personal relations appear to be more sincere than our media glitz and hype allow us to act. The muddy hands and bent back of the manual laborer should be compared to the sly eyes and grimy consciences of our masters of business avarice. Religious values may underlie some of the obvious visual variations between East and West. This seemingly eternal enigma could rest upon the essential differences between Buddhism and Christianity.

This pragmatic and oversimplified appraisal of Buddhism leaves many unknowns but all seem to emphasize compassion and self denial. The religion tolerates no castes, proposes twenty-six heavenly rewards, and is opposed to Brahmanism, from which it grew. Originating in northern India, it entered China about the time of Christ and then traveled to Burma, Ceylon, and Japan. Tibetan Buddhism grew through heirarchichal priesthoods, such as the Red and the Yellow Hats, and a large complex system of monasteries.

In Tibet, Mahayana Buddhism comingled with an earlier animism. The monks were called lamas and the religion was Lamaism. The first order of monks began in the mid eighth century and these celibate orders came to elect their religious leader, the Dalai Lama, as a result of direct reincarnation and through the body of an infant selected by the lamas, apparently at random, from the laity. The Dalai Lama resided in Lhasa until the mid twentieth century when the Chinese invaded Tibet and he was required to flee to India where he still maintains his religious status. The Chinese have destroyed many of the monasteries and allow only token occupancy in the rest.

Buddhist people are portrayed here as a recognizable segment of humankind that has great consistency, and can therefore represent at least one major aspect of religious character, particularly as it includes moral and ethical beliefs. But how do we judge character from a photographic image? Can it be done? Perhaps, but underlying every visual interpretation, especially where the vagaries of religion are involved, lie layers of accumulated judgments and these must be weighed and reweighed as each scene is judged. Current conditions and beliefs must be balanced simultaneously.

How should we judge a person's moral qualities, his origin, and social evolution? Do we sit in the skin of the person in the photograph and relate his values to our own, or should we compare what we think we see to a more abstract truth? Certainly moral and mental qualities distinguish an individual, or a group of homogenious individuals as in a race or religion. Mental and moral attributes that are strongly developed are unusual and create a distinguishing character. Character grew from the Greek word describing a tool for marking or making something distinctive. A mark of distinction is easily observed, provided that we know why it is distinct. Are we distinguishable from others in the vicinity, from our kind, or from all men? There are obviously degrees of character or distinction. We can be distinctive by means of hair dye, deformity, good deeds, or heinous acts, all based upon accidents. It is not simply being different that reveals human character but the consistent intention to achieve a transcendent purpose, that guarantees character, either in a person or the things he makes.

Moral and ethic do not mean the same thing. A moral person may not be ethical, as when a Roman Catholic priest gives the last rites of the church to a venal sinner. An ethical surgeon may not be moral, as when he needlessly extends the life of a suffering and terminally ill patient. Morals develop from within the individual while ethics involves the acceptance of what a group considers proper. Morals are choices made by the individual while ethics is little more than compliance with a set of rules agreed upon by others. As we attempt to evaluate a visual scene we must apply personal principles of right and wrong as sanctioned by our inner conscience. Whether the act being performed is legal or approved by society is an ethical issue. Ethics deals with good and bad through a generalized set of principles and social beliefs that determine how everyone should behave. Ethics outlines principles of conduct that emanate from without. Morals occur from within. Morals represent compacts between me and my conscience.

The shadings of right and wrong can be very subtle. As we observe human efforts we weigh them through our own experiences. The moral rules of right conduct, within ourselves, and ethics established by society are related but almost never the same. All of us are concerned with what others think, but a person of character will defer what he is told is right to his own independent judgment. We may choose to differ with what has been, with what others have thought. Standards, including virtue and vice, are in constant change, so each of us is responsible for the innumerable daily imputations that we accept. Our associations cannot be separated from what we think and how we judge the visual and physical world around us. Our judgments are not only important when they involve major issues, such as life and death, for we are just as responsible for the minutia of everyday human contacts, a wink here, a frown there.

Ethical and moral challenges are quite different for the practicing Christian, Buddhist, and agnostic. A Buddhist in southern Burma and one in Tokyo have the same religion but not the same values. Their interpretations of moral responsibilities are shaped by very different societal forces. Social responsibility to a poor Burmese rice farmer living within the Golden Triangle is not the same as that of an industrial worker in Tokyo. An enigma to one is a clear truth to the other. One sees no sin in the production and sale of opium poppies while the other is not concerned with the harmful effects of economic subjugation. Which is more sinful, the production of a pain deadening narcotic or the waste of flimsy, limited life, annual car models? Is the sin in a thing's production or in its use? The principles of conduct governing individuals and groups vary greatly, as do the ethical and moral content of the following photographs.

As we observe the human face and physique what is the basis of our evaluation? Do we limit our judgments to personal experience and the mythos of our own society? If our interpretations are more catholic, how do we confront our own unknowns? Do we seek to determine individual opportunity and intention or do we attribute all human accomplishments to such criteria as the size and ethnicity of the group? The pure and the social sciences obviously differ in this matter. One seeks progress through individual revelations and the other is concerned with collective truths.

Remember, as you view the following vignettes of people that you should test your interpretations by assuming opposing conditions and meanings. You should concern yourself with both differences and similarities, the instructive and the insidious, the insightful and the merely scenic. Later, as you review all of the photographs separately from the text, and as you relate photographs from other groupings, your opinions will change, often either enlarging or collapsing. If your opinions do not change, then you are simply not looking.

Photo 56, Bowling Green, Cape Point to Capetown, Republic of South Africa, 1981, is an ocean front facility located alongside flanking mountains as they confront the Atlantic Ocean on the southwest coast of Cape Province. Whether representing comfortable retirees or the clinging vestiges of colonialism, a group of carefully outfitted senior citizens is obviously enjoying the good life. Their collective exclusivity, reminiscent of the British Raj in India, "a race destined to govern and subdue," is here receiving payment for accrued services. It is a quaint irony that the very same type of colonials were responsible for the destruction of the great European empires. Their afternoon gins and tonic, lawn games, and supercilious gossip, all while in appropriate costume, brought about the ultimate downfall of the colonies. Or was it simply their hauteur and contempt for those who made their luxuries possible? While seldom actually abusive to those whose lives they so self-righteously dominated, they commanded a distinction quite impossible for them to have at home. Their games seldom involved physical contact, but, as here, utilized calculating but not wearying skills. These purveyors of advancing technology and western ways were fastidious organizers who partially adapted to native ways while assuming long-reaching control. They often assumed physical risks and underwent discomforts, but in the end they demanded excessive personal rewards.

The assumption of undue status, as if ordained by providence, whether achieved through trade, religion, gunpowder, or narcotics was seemingly predestined: the right of civilized man to dictate to the less advanced aborigine. A series of almost fraternal national orders developed in Europe to present themselves as God's other chosen people. With pomp and power they undertook to subdue cultures in many ways their superiors. By historic accident their institutions, weapons, and cohesiveness were superior and their religions apparently more understanding of brutal excesses. Colonial powers became working models for the application of ruthless extractive power while native peoples were enslaved in their own lands.

So it was, and is now, in Tibet. *Photo 57, Tibetan Exile, Darjeeling, India, 1985*, shows a Tibetan expatriate living in a refugee camp. The memorable face of this leather worker seems to have assumed the same colors and texture as the animal skins that she works. There is a sustaining dignity here that shines around the treasured western sunglasses. She may have been evicted from her historic home because of here belief, but without sham she has turned suffering into contemplation. Her Lamaist beliefs have been her salvation. She survives, representative of a movement opposing aggression, with calm determination.

Photo 58, Yak Caravan near Zhanang, Tibet, 1988, lets the viewer ponder that attraction of high places. The land is arid and barren, the seasons deceptive, breathing difficult, and the exertion to survive is great; but there is a special dignity in such remote places with their luxury of distance between humans. The Himalayan highlands are a home to the most serviceable beast on earth; or so the yak has become in Tibet. The yak serves as tractor, dairy, truck, mobile home, companion, fabric source, ceremonial deity, packing plant, and mobile all-purpose storehouse of supplies. Tibetans anticipated Henry Ford in utilizing even the honk in the hog. Nothing is wasted, not even its urine or manure. The former is used as a cleaning fluid and the latter as firewood. Beyond these radiant facts, this all-purpose animal, with its long hair, is amiable, hardworking, and easily directed. In its own very special way, the yak is also beautiful. Here a group of animals vitalizes a dreary wasteland as they transport necessities of life.

Beauty, even high in the mountains, cannot be taken for granted. It must be recorded and at times transformed by people. This does not occur by accident. *Photo 59, Drawing Class, Thimphu, Bhutan, 1989*, records the colorful apparel of a group of Bhutanese children in their art school class. Like children everywhere, one is less attentive, but probably more adventurous than the others. He is not yet tamed, broken to the plow of society. The group is here being socially conditioned, and while this may seem an outrage against their individual creative natures, it is essential for the state. Ultimately, great artists break away from tradition, but in their early years facility must be patiently learned. The iconoclast must await his attack, and here the sweet unattentive face of a child may foretell of creativity yet to come. In our ritualized urban world, conformity can become a necessary precedent for success, an essential ingredient for acceptibility, but some will always find opportunities for new and creative departures.

While Buddhism is very tolerant and seemingly gentle, its demand for self denial has not permitted many forms of social and economic change to occur. Buddhist counties, except for the recent surges in Japan, Taiwan, and Korea, have produced few advances in this century. The age of pure faith, along with the age of pure reason, have given way to an age of believing, or information as we call it; believing without religious prejudice! *Photo 60, Buddhist Monks, near Thazi, Burma, 1987*, stand in the cantankerous openings of an old building. They are conscious of their dramatic setting and have undoubtedly planned this pose. These rather melancholy ruins are a proper setting for the self denial so deeply imbedded in Buddhist thought. The subtle colors of their robes, against the weathered wooden siding, associate their beliefs with suffering and the cessation of desire. Youthful faith is seen throughout Burma and is another aspect of Buddhism. Faith has many such faces.

Photo 61, Devout Faith, Tashilhunpo Monastery, Xigaze, Tibet, 1988, records an elderly worshipper of unusual facial structure, with sentient eyes and a composure that reflects an approach to nirvana. For those in advanced age religion is often all that is left to give purpose to life. This weathered face, along with a few unmanageable whiskers, reassures us that there can be sweetness in the aging process.

In northern Thailand, *Photo 62, Proposition, Karen Hill Tribes, Lampoon to Tak, Thailand, 1987*, another set of values, a different ethos, is in sway. A maturing child presents all of her wares, as mercantile Bangkok exerts its influence. Tribes such as this child's, traditional traffickers in narcotics, have been sealed off from their usual ways and left with little to sustain them except the beneficence of the central government and the sale of trinkets shown here. Inherited characteristics may exist and make us wonder whether moral turpitude has genetic beginnings. A way of life in one place of power far removed from another can destroy customs that have been stable for generations. In this picture we perceive a demonstration of raw international economic power. Depraved narcotics users living thousands of miles away have destroyed a way of life besides their own. The compellingly wistful smile of this child begs forgiveness. Her transient appeal may indicate that Buddhism is her only escape from the irrational distant forces that dictate her future.

Today in Tibet the ancient monasteries are in ruins or are ghost towns. The ideology remains but much of the tradition of Lamaism has been destroyed, never to be restored. *In Photo 63, Caucus of Buddhist Monks, Drepung Monastery, Lhasa, Tibet, 1988*, we see a common sight. Ordained monks continue to recite prayers, intone chants and sound great horns and drums, but their social function has been destroyed by the invading Chinese. Who is in the wrong, the overzealous Chinese in their quest for growth, raw materials, and a unified national purpose, or the monks in their monasteries where in the past society was forced to support thousands upon thousands of unproductive celibates whose only function was prayer? Archaic conditions exist everywhere, yet the monks, such as those seen here, seem happy and intellectually active. They realize that they oppose the overwhelming mass of a closely knit state that demands a complete change in language and customs. The very soul of Tibetan culture is their religion, and it is critically at risk. The traditional mix of an omniscient priesthood and a rather servile populace is being replaced by a foreign militarist government, a resisting but impotent priesthood, and a still servile populace.

The people of the world live in recurring cycles of change where religion and power frequently exchange places. Cruel and autocratic ways exist at either extreme, and as we seek substance within the visual images of our time, the significance of religion must be weighed against its costs. For as Nietzche wrote: "The strangest and most evil spirits have so far advanced humanity the most; they have always rekindled the drousing passions . . ."

From the green, green bowling green we have moved through the dry, gray austerity of the high country, to the rich and exotic people and plants of Southeast Asia, and then back again to thoughtful monks considering the future of man, or of a pretty girl. People are indeed curious, either one at a time or in groups, and their religious beliefs are even more abstruse, as we will see as we investigate some of the physical expressions of religious faith.

X   RELIGION-FAITH AND VISUAL PLACES

The perennial search for individual wholeness, mentioned earlier, requires resolution of the conflict between our rational-romantic duality. One seems real and predictable, while the other is indistinct and effervescent. One involves such things as practicality and efficiency, and the other simply questions and originates. Over thirty-five thousand years ago a cultural explosion seems to have simultaneously occurred in many places on our planet. Archaeologists have found delicately made stone and bone figurines and other cult or religious artifacts from this remote paleolithic age. Why did men in many parts of the world, isolated from one another, suddenly become so concerned with faith and continuity in so short a period of time? No one knows.

Faith is a more encompassing word than religion. Both are deeply seated within the human conscience, and man has seemed incapable of living without them at any stage of his social evolution. We all know that life is too short and that our span on earth is equivalent to a momentary bomb blast that diffuses, irradiates, and then destroys our beliefs, accomplishments, and aspirations. For the last thirty-five millenia, man has enlarged the meaning of symbols depicting adoration and continuity. Today, we refer to such objects as religious artifacts or structures. Some are reverential and some only represent material efforts to extend the memory of an individual or belief.

Faith is something believed or adhered to; it involves a strong sense of trust and confidence but it does not demand unquestioning belief without need of proof. To have faith does not require prejudice and the acceptance of forcefully directed opinions. Such convictions belong within the sphere of religion and not within the scope of faith.

Many aspects of life are not measurable, certainly all of those involving quality, so it is not surprising that many subjective generalizations are mingled within what we call religion. People seem to prefer to group their opinions regarding our: *from whence, why,* and *to where.* We create systems of devotion, supreme beings, and explanations of existence under the generic title of religion. Organized religions are an expression of the romantic mind and by definition can only exist within organized groups. Religion's earliest meaning in the western world was to bind together, to unite. Religions are held responsible for defining the standards of spiritual and practical life, as found collectively acceptable by their congregations.

The hard protective outer covering of a turtle, is a carpace. It is a word that we should remember. The "hard shelled" Southern Baptist, the Orthodox Jew, and many other aggressive, proselytes revel in their carpacious exclusivity. If their ominous tenets are ignored, fear, dread and pain lie ahead. Awe, the reverent wonder that always includes fear, infuses religion's sly instructions and then extends into the realms of personal, business, and political relations. The welfare of the religious group usually transcends individual good. Perhaps this is why "people who like people" are so lucky, particularly when they can convert others to the advantages of their group.

Faith and religion carry instructions implanted within our subconscious mind. They have enormous influence upon our likes and dislikes, our so-called tastes, and they can only be altered through the most persistent effort and objective analysis. This search for truth involves subjective forces and symbols that we hardly recognize. The bases of such sensations as fear, joy, dismay, and ecstacy must be isolated and made subject to predictable reason.

The religious beliefs of the Mayan civilization are unknown, but the striking arrangements of their ceremonial centers were obviously based upon spatial and astronomical relations. *Photo 64, Temple of the Cross, Palenque Ruins, Chiapas, Mexico, 1984,* reveals an intensity of green that is common to tropical rain forests. The soft contrast between verdant plants, seeming to drift away to a misty horizon, and the conjectured religious rituals conducted here in the past creates a romantic illusion of the unknown, with an expectation that further investigation will reveal even greater mysteries. Does the strong sense of religious purpose recorded here arise from intuitions from the past, or is it only the diffused light, season, and time of day, acting upon our retina? Is the rather ominous environment indicative of past calamities, or does it record a deeply religious and hopeful sacrament? Does the thought that these people may have consumed the blood of their captives of war influence our opinions of this ceremonial place? In cultural contrast is the Christian eucharist pagan and bloodthirsty? Is the attraction of this picture the result of the ancient works of man or the recent works of nature? We often seem to judge the unknown, including religions, by gross assumptions and often by what we erroneously feel.

In *Photo 65, Schwedagon Pagoda, Rangoon, Burma, 1987,* another act of religious faith permeates a circular plaza that contains scores of smaller pagodas, stupas, chaitas, and memorials that girdle this enormous gold encrusted Schwedagon. This large central dome or masonry tumulus contains some of the human remains of Buddha. The profusion of smaller stupas, chortens, topes, pagodas, and other memorial religious structures are of many types and represent a variety of religious purposes and epochs. The multi-roofed pagodas originated in what is now Nepal. Many of these emblematic monuments are sarcophagi and contain the ashes of venerated monks, while others are simply objects of symbolic reverence.

The multiplicity of creatively contrasting shapes, materials, and finishes, all watched over by the enormous bell-shaped, central gold dome, create a many faceted congruity that may be unmatched by any other religious structure on earth. Elevated above the surround, Schwedagon has a jewel-like quality of incomparable richness and refinement. To the Burmese Buddhist, Schwedagon must represent a museum of salvation, the ultimate attainment of both beauty and reality; at the same time it allows a hopeful respite from worldly cares. Whatever the religious connotations within the beholder, the photograph is vitalized by the afternoon sun dancing across the mass of strange, wet shapes. In the afterglow of a monsoon the mystery of life in this strange place assumes a rich visual life that is all its own.

Photo 66, Wat Nari Poonchai Temple Classroom, Chiang Mai, Thailand, 1987, is obviously an invasion of religious privacy. The photograph, resulting from a random camera placement within a protective screen, candidly divulges the organization and instruction within a Buddhist compound. A youthful environment mixes lay and religious instruction, much as in a Roman Catholic catechism class. The monks, novices, and neophytes in their saffron and yellow robes are learning to understand the essence of Buddhahood and its earthly benefits. Mixing conventional reason with the folklore of pantheistic mysticism, amid the chanting of mantras, the precepts of a highly organized religion are carried forward to another generation. Ultimate mysteries are reduced to firm beliefs and fixed religious allegiances. In this way the phenomenological base of this special faith is impregnated in young and receptive minds.

Photo 67, Making A Mandala, Tashilhumpo Monastery, Xigaze, Tibet, 1988, is a record of an enthralled meeting held to design a symbolic representation of the magic circle. These Tantric Buddhist monks are collectively, and apparently in a state of exaltation, attempting to infuse a manmade object with magical and symbolic qualities. Mandalas usually subdivide a circle into symmetrical divisions with figures or deities in the center. They are used during meditation and have doctrinal significance. They often represent vengeful deities of great knowledge. Concentration and participation are recorded here in an event of great meaning. The scene exudes expectation, togetherness, and brotherly caring. Elders work alongside their juniors as they collectively attempt to decipher and give new meaning to the circle of life. Few sights are more engaging than where a group is seen working to a common purpose and is engrossed in an activity beyond any selfish advantage. A radiant sense of good intentions moves from the image to the viewer.

Even Buddhist monasteries outlive their usefulness. *Photo 68, Abandoned Borne Monastery, near Paro, Bhutan, 1989*, records a burned monastery long in disuse. Around its base farmers have built their houses and now till the formerly sacred grounds. However, prayer flags still fly and pilgrims still visit the holy place. A sense of attachment to the soil and the natural cycles of nature enlivens a once remote defensive position straddling a ridge in the middle of a rich valley. The colors are muted, and the farm houses seem to grow from the earth as geologic phenomena.

Photo 69, Church Courtyard, Izamal, Yucatan, Mexico, 1990, records the deteriorating remains of a building and a religion that wantonly, if with religious ecstacy and fervor, attempted the total destruction of another culture and faith. Symbolically, the arch is everywhere, and the native corbel is unused. The photograph contrasts the building of Roman Catholic voids with the earlier pagan pyramids; the use of contained interior spaces at the expense of nature on the exterior. The church shown here is built from, and upon, the remains of Mayan religious pyramids that reveled in the stars and the infinite universe. This Catholic building is now itself ineffective and all but abandoned. Unkempt and poorly maintained, it is developing the same allure of abandonment that its pyramidal progenitors enjoyed, before their malicious destruction. Self-righteous religious beliefs, particularly Christian beliefs, have justified torture, extortion, and almost all conceivable forms of induced fear.

In this photograph the ominous storm clouds in the background contrast, and give vigor to, the dull and repetitious shapes of the arch. The viewer is drawn between the writhing tensions of the El Greco-like background and the saccharine circular repetitions in the foreground. There is tension and drama here as the scene awaits the arrival of a righteous executioneer.

Quite another set of emotions comes to mind as you enter *Photo 70, Churches Within Kremlin Walls, Moscow, Russia, 1978*. The religious connotations expressed by the conventionalized visual streamers of light radiating from above, striking the golden domes before the dark storm clouds, is not borne out by existing realities. These are no longer religious structures, and the faith that they serve today is of another kind. The sense of ecstatic religious expectations that must have been felt by the original designers and builders has lost its purpose in everything but momentary quirks of nature, such as that shown here. The exhaltation felt in this unexpected display of radiant light cannot convey the rapturous emotions that once engaged the original believers. The silhouettes remain just as striking, the gold dome profiles are just as exotic, the crucifixes are just as confidently near the sky, but the infusion of a living belief is gone; in its place only an ill-at-ease anxiety remains.

Is all of this just imagination? Would I have seen and felt things differently if the Tsar still lived? I believe that I would, not that I believe in the original religious purpose more than its current secular use, but that the heart, the spirit has been removed and only the body remains. The essentials of the original place would alter my perceptions even as the restored stage set denigrates the original reality. So many churches within the central compound of atheism mock their origins. Religion and its symbols, from mandalas for visualizing the dreamer's striving for unity, to these gilded, onion-shaped domes with their expressions of religious prowess, power, and adoration are institutionalized symbols that we are supposed to rely upon, that relegate and bind people and their values together. Whether to draw and drink human blood or to unify and strengthen the beliefs of an ethnically and religiously diverse nation, formal religion demands compliance with collective rules. Such allegiances will always be useful to leaders. Their virtue for individuals is more questionable.

Is this gracious goodness that burst from within the clouds and strikes the gilded domes within the Kremlin, or is it the light of truth, or mere reformation and good will? But here, we are only discussing the symbolism of an innocent act of nature, whereas our ultimate interpretation may be based upon early training when our minds were more resilient and receptive. Faith, trust, and religion seem to be randomly braided within our brains. These are powerful forces that alter our lives because we cannot resist their appeal.

Spirit has long been claimed in the name of faith and related religion but is, I believe, something distinctly different. Even animals have it. It activates both our mind and our reactions, physical as well as emotional. Spirit has been described as a kind of breath that infiltrates the blood and animates the body, even creating character from peculiarities. Spirit intoxicates and lets us feel inspiration, that involuntary drawing in of our breath or intellect, when something compels an unusual sense of truth, place, or motivation. We recognize the vitality, or spirit of the place, as it enlivens us with an intangible sense of the unusual or the profound.

This spirit within us can inspire feelings of ecstacy and rapture unequaled by any religious motive. At times, when we comprehend new associations or explicit new relations, we sense a special kind of inspiration. Spirit then is not a state of being beyond explanation, but rather is very much within our capacity for individual reason, a powerful exaltation and delight. When we recognize the spirit of a place, it lets us realize the wholeness of our existence and fills our entire being with a newfound sense of significance, joy, and calm.

The spirit of a place is, for me, revealed in *Photo 71, Shack, Ghoom Monastery, near Darjeeling, India, 1985*, where a small house, no more than a shack, is located at the edge of a precipice. Buried in shadow, the foreground acts as a supporting foil for life-giving sunlight as it strikes and seems to support the enclosed lookout. I cannot fully explain the satisfaction, the fulfillment, the contentment, and the lasting gratification that I feel. The vision satisfies a deep need or recollection, while *Photo 72, Hillside Lookout, Lake Palace, Udaipur, India, 1985*, achieves a similar response upon very different terrain. The slight rise, or hill, topped by a small house surrounded by scattered trees could be located in many places from central Texas to the foothills of the Andes. The general character of the scene is undistinguished but displays a wanton quality that is, to me, magic. Some unknown agency, opposing classic design logic, has built at the summit of a small hill and thereby achieved great distinction. My reaction

may be based upon the relation of the mountains in the background or the lake in the foreground, or it could have commenced with the magic of a moment in time when the light was reflected from the knoll. I believe, though, that it occurs because someone came to a completely undistinguished location and lent the place the miracle of his own spirit.

At another extreme is *Photo 73, Tannery, Mikness, Morocco, 1982*. The spirit of this rank and malodorous place will always remain in my memory. The scene achieves a fetid character that is conclusive, an enclosed hell in an abandoned abattoire. The hapless existence of the workers, seen against the evil composts of dead skin and flesh, is supported by the overcast sky, by a general disregard for minimum human amenities, and by the disorder of an ultimately unclean environment. Yet there is in this visual experience a spirit of the place that could not be duplicated or allayed. I returned to this photograph time after time before its final selection. This is probably because most scenes that I chose were in some way idealistic. This photograph could represent a deep rooted protest against slick prettiness and scenic pretensions.

None of my choices was more idealistic than *Photo 74, Reflections, Konigssee, Austria, 1984*, where visual perfection, in a generally accepted way, meets all of our expectations. Here in the Alps, not far from Hitler's Berchtesgaden and Eagle's Nest, this tranquil scene, with its mirrorlike reflections, assesses a people and a culture. Calm, consistent, and approaching everyone's visual ideal, the scene conveys a perfection almost beyond human tolerance. The cool colors and bright sun create the same responses as looking at a beautiful mermaid. She is just too perfect for her own good, or anyone else's. "Pretty" lacks the body of real beauty.

Photo 75, Meteora Monastery, Kalambaka, Greece, 1990, is at the other end of another set of extreme values. Great weathered stone masses rear up to support medieval monasteries that serve as an ultimate form of human isolation. Begun by hermits, these refuges from society represent feelings that are latent in all of us. Men came here to think, to regenerate, and to gain perspective. The power of these great washed stone outcroppings seems to oppose even nature itself and may have been subconsciously associated with the original hermits' desire to stand fast, while the rest of mankind, as they saw it, flowed aimlessly past. Whether founded in religious fervor or through fear and trepidation, these defensive retreats remain as visual bulwarks against social change, whether the tyranny of government or of religion.

Located in an unproductive and undesirable geologic area, the hermits removed themselves to the equivalent of today's abandoned automobile in an overgrown junkyard and built their own idiosyncratic world. To achieve a purer freedom the monks chose this extreme and hazardous form of physical isolation. An extraordinary visual environment ensued as unimaginable challenges were met and overcome. The tenacity of their efforts remains clearly expressed and lies at the heart of the attraction of these remote constructions.

In *Photo 76, Temple of a Thousand Columns, Chichen Itza, Yucatan, Mexico, 1982*, an arid and completely flat plain is overviewed by itinerant, fluffy, white clouds. The Mayan and Toltec ruins are not exciting from this view, but the wind-blown grass creates a moving skin for the clouds to visually powder. Sandwiched between moving grass and transiting clouds, the mysterious precolumbian ruins assume a mystery all their own. A visual moment captivates the spirit and the viewer with a serene feeling for the everlasting quality of this human achievement. Located miles from modern urban life, these remains of a primitive ceremonial center once accommodated thousands. Today archaeologists and horticulturists have created an impressive, park-like setting to honor those who once inhabited the rocky terrain. We may miss the flashing plumage of their pagan ceremonies, but we will always admire the wisdom with which they sited their buildings. The Mayans found salvation through an effort to make their buildings last, and this could not have been accidental. I wonder if we, the citizens of the twentieth century, will be able to say that we matched their efforts when our culture is of an equal age.

Swedes have an interesting sense of humor. *Photo 77, Window Display, Stockholm, Sweden, 1986*, contains a decorative Leda joining other merchandise of fantasy and delusive appearance to create an exotic shopper-stopping apparition. The window demands an emotional response. It simply cannot be ignored, and neither can the items that are so outrageously related. This is a visual event with spirit and an ambivalence that can serve as a catalog of possibilities for the curious mind.

All of these photographs, as metaphors of life and hope, are related to man's history of cruelty, sacrifice, and death. The spilling of blood, so well recorded in religious history, demands recollection. Against this sensibility we should discuss death and memorials in other lights, for they are closely related, as man seeks unity with nature and the forces of his innermost being. All of us want to be remembered, to achieve more than animals slinking across the stage of life.

The origins of primal social rituals may lie in religion, but the physical symbols that we individually leave, so often recorded in battered physical things, have a pertinence that must also be recognized. Burial monuments and memorials often tell us more about cultures than their words and religious mythologies. Death is universal and everlasting and the way that we dispose of our bodies is socially revealing.

XI DEATH-CEMETERIES-MEMORIALS

The poet William Cowper wrote: "Death is neither the most formidable, or the most comfortable thing we have in prospect." This rather optimistic statement comes from a man who suffered from a religious mania where morbid guilt, and intermittent insanity overwhelmed him. The grim fact is that pain and death probably preoccupy more human thought than any other subject. The insidiousness of death occupies much of our time, dominates religious thought and is evident in even our most unconscious and commonplace decisions.

Death is difficult to accept, for mental conceptions grow through developing past experiences and memory. We cannot conceive of our own death in this way. We may realize that dying is the end of life and our animal functions, but how can it be the end of the comprehension and thought that we have always taken for granted? Perhaps it is not so much that we dread death, or the cessation of life, as we fear oblivion, the end of our mental activities, our existence on earth.

The realities and ideals that we have developed to live by, our conceptions of honor and right, our very reasons for being, are cut off and suddenly gone. How can such waste occur with an all-knowing and supreme power in charge? As we confront death in others, we can glimpse their responses but not their actual feelings. We can analyze the interpretations of more knowledgeable scientists, artists, and philosophers, but we must await actuality to really know. Therefore death can only be a mental construction, an imaginary condition. Any real understanding of this irreversible moment lies in the future. In the interim we can only seek understanding through the observation of people and their customs. Death and its many responsive rites are indeed strange. Both are unfamiliar, astonishing, and to the dying, ultimately abnormal. In death there is always a sense of wonder, a feeling of disbelief. The strange sensations that we feel in the presence of death are indescribable. For the sentient human there is no accommodation to such a brutal and savage act. All of us know that death should only involve someone else's life. We deserve better.

Biologically speaking, death of tissue cells within the body constitutes a microcosm that is very similar to the death of an individual when it happens within a society. During life, our tissue cells are constantly dying and being renewed. Even after the death of the body, as a whole, these tissues survive for some time. It is much the same with families and societies. The influence of the individual continues to affect the present even after death occurs. For the living the changes that occur as the result of the death of a near one are traumatic. Memory can be temporarily lost and normal balances destroyed.

Through the ages death rites have sought compromises between the requirements of physical sanitation and the survivor's emotional needs. The cult of immortality evolved and is basic to the Christian and Islamic faiths, while Judaism is ambivalent on the subject. Buddhists and Hindus find immortality unnecessary and prefer reincarnation. Life after death can be an appealing but confusing thought. Life under what conditions? Each religion seems to offer its own answers.

Animism, the principle of a vital force permeating the world, involves a nonmaterial power that is separate and distinct from matter and is associated with all living things. Animists believe that this force, equal to a living soul, exists even in inanimate objects as well as in the world of nature. They believe that the soul is separate and distinct from matter, much the same as spiritualism differs from materialism. The animist's entire faith is based upon unseen spiritual forces. Polytheism rests heavily upon animism, and among native cultures such as those in Mexico, Peru, and Finland there is a continuing animistic foundation to their external Christian trappings.

A later but related doctrine is that of Animatism that seems to ascribe psychic qualities to inanimate objects. While such tenets may be scientifically unsupportable, they have great value for original thinking and creative activities. A recent architect asked himself as he designed buildings: what does this space, or function, want to be, want to do? Ascribing desire to objects, as we look upon or within them, can provide creative responses within the viewer. This can apply equally well to an interpretation of physical symbols or other less calculated triggering mechanisms. Certainly as we look at images or scenes that contain human beings we try to interpret their thoughts, their condition, as we shape our own. This attribution of thought and action to inanimate things, even representations, is offensive to many religions, but it has been an integral part of the creative process for centuries. Why else do we paint tigers on fighter planes, name trains, and refer to the sex of ships?

The first problem confronting any religious interpretation must be the nature of existence. As interpreted above, Animatism and Spiritualism are chiefly concerned with the vital but unseen forces of the soul. Pantheism usually denies the existence of an individual human soul, but does allow transmigration. Materialism even denies the soul's existence. Christians sometimes describe the soul as "the thinking life of man." It is interesting that psychology based its original name upon the "science of the soul."

Immortality has been described as having many faces and rewards. Protestant Christians visualize a state of individual bliss with God seemingly available on a personal basis. Roman Catholics can ultimately achieve the same joys as their Protestant neighbors but must first submit to a detour through their special purgatory. Both utilize the same imagery and, like Islam, promise eternal bliss for the virtuous. In the opposite condition, God and the Church condemn the evil usurper of their laws to endless pain and the fire of hell.

Throughout history heavens and hells have been described with great variety and creativity from Elysian Fields, at the edge of the Greek world and providing for heroes favored by the Gods, to Valhalla, the paradise of Norsemen slain in battle. The rewards of heaven and hell, including such special interest groups as these, vary greatly, but before burial and the claiming of their individual rewards the insanitary remains must be disposed of.

The ritual of burial, or disposal, the separation of the living from the dead, has many cultural variations. Whether the body is committed to burial, exposure, or cremation, the corpse is removed from the immediate world of the living. The act of depositing it in the ground or burning it in the atmosphere, in theory and belief, returns the body to nature from whence it came. The practice goes to the edge of recorded history, but the name cemetery, as a burial ground set aside for this sole purpose, apparently came from the Roman catacombs and described a "dormitory for the dead." Burial ceremonies are worldwide and spring from uniform emotional needs. One of the more interesting interpretations of the burial ceremony occurred among American Indians who celebrated the conclusion of war by the burying of a tomahawk, their symbol of death.

But, the simple necessity of disposing of the body was not enough to satisfy the living. The perpetuation of the memory of the dead, their love, acts and accomplishments, by the living, was a universal need. The desire to physically preserve a memory became a compulsion and commemorative acts and symbols were devised. Memory was stimulated through both celebrations and physical symbols that are often combined to provide protection from oblivion.

Photo 78, Cemetery, Izamal, Yucatan, Mexico, 1982, is one of four photographs used here to relate death, disposal, cemeteries, and remembrance. This small rural cemetery is both more and less than it seems. Crosses and crucifixes atop the tombs seem to serve notice of a Christian burial ground, yet other symbols and arrangements make it clear that animism and a pantheon of earlier gods is still very much alive. Each tomb represents the personal efforts of loved ones to express a continuing concern and devotion for the departed through their own handiwork. Here I sense a place where the living and the dead meet often, and on equal terms. Softness and the remembrance of special moments are evident everywhere, and death is not accepted as a "fait accompli." The intimate grouping of tombs, abstractly resembling a village, presents an evocative epilogue to an understood and appreciated life of service. This is a happy place of sunlight, soft breezes, and sweet memories.

In *Photo 79, Bagmati River Cremation Ghats and Leprosarium, Pashupatinath, Nepal, 1985*, another aspect of the dance of death is seen. A leprosarium in the background and a hospice for the destitute and dying overlook the river with its cremation platforms. The entrance to the temple is alongside. Is it accident that here again we sense the gloomy and foreboding Stygian Shore? Is this Nepalese River Styx another reincarnation of the common folklore of the ages? Here death often terminates the agony of terrible deformity and is a welcome occurrence. Bicyles are washed while the crematory fire is kindled and the approaching participants to the event look on. There is little seeming cause for remembrance present; the greatest need is for release. Yet, here too the sun shines, and bright colors pervade the drab and gloomy environment that is so involuntarily grim.

Photo 80, Tarajaland Burial Crypts, Sulawesi, Indonesia, 1987, explores the cliffside burial crypts of the descendents of ancient Chinese wanderers. Animists, these people are farmers with large families living together in compounds. When death occurs, extensive burial preparations begin. Large ceremonial burials are common and last for days. They are expensive, the cooperative venture of an extended family of relatives. Often the corpse is stored for months, usually in the loft of the residence, while funds are assembled, festivities planned, and the tomb carved and readied for use. Special facilities, including an entire village with houses, grandstands, and pavilions are constructed for the single funeral ceremony. When the auspicious time comes, there are often hundreds of family, guests, and onlookers. Ceremonial dances and formalities last for days as the proceedings are meticulously choreographed, rehearsed, and anachronistically recorded on video tape. Scared bullocks and fattened pigs are consumed in a carnival-like atmosphere while the casket remains in view. At last the corpse is removed and entombed in an elevated stone crypt. Nearby, also carved into the face of the cliff, is a balcony-like niche holding lifelike effigies of the occupants of the adjacent tombs.

The corpse has been disposed of, the psychological needs of the survivors tended, and a figurative memorial has been put in place to represent the continuation of the family unit. *Photo 81, Burial Effigies, Tarajaland, Sulawesi, Indonesia, 1987*, shows the gray and lifelike plaster effigies of a family of the dead, in a comparable cliffside burial wall. It is significant, I think, that these burial places with their representations of the dead are located in the middle of the rice fields where the survivors work. Here death is not a cataclysmic event, and the survivor's commemorative efforts are not intended for everyone, or forever. They are intended to allow the dead to continue to participate in the daily affairs of the living. These are true memorials, acts of continued knowing and caring.

Memorials representing larger and more historic concerns such as those of monarchs and religious leaders apparently require more massive expressions. These have included the efforts of thousands such as those of Egypt's pharaohs and India's conquering moguls. *Photo 82, Colossi of Memnon, across Nile River from Karnak, Egypt, 1980*, overlooks the center-poise of ancient Egyptian culture. Seventy feet high, these vandalized visages were originally intended to preserve remembrances associated with the life and destroyed funerary temple of Amenhotep IV. As one of the elaborate burial precincts of Egypt's pharaohs, the area now epitomizes desolation, rancor, and destruction. Such malicious damage makes the viewer ponder what malevolent hate was responsible for creating such shadowed monsters. As guardians, in their seated hauteur, they are now more grotesquely fearsome than they ever could have been before their tortures.

Photo 83, Supposed Location, Colossus of Rhodes, Isle of Rhodes, Greece, 1980, presents a powerful contrast to the last photograph. In this calm and mistbound location there once stood a heroic statue of Apollo that is said to have been over one hundred feet in height and between whose legs Greek ships and men-of-war entered and left civilization. According to myth it was destroyed by an earthquake. It is touching that this massive symbol of a departed culture was so elegantly replaced by the refined, but non-competitive, shapes of a male and a female deer. Separated as they are, by a water gate, their isolated relationship joins with an almost lost horizon to create the sense of a gently guarded, but protected, port. The Rhodian Apollo was one of the seven wonders of the ancient world and may have been quantitatively appropriate for the time, but accommodating my animistic instincts I prefer the qualitative essence represented by the expectant shapes of a doe and a buck standing atop their unifying columns. Protective time settles in, along with the dusk, as sound floats across the channel.

A less known and obvious memorial, *Photo 84, Arch at Labna, Yucatan, Mexico, 1982*, consists of a well-proportioned corbelled vault that raises the possibility that circular arches may have been conceived but not accepted by these subtle aestheticians. The decorative patterns, shown here, create rich and variable shadows in the sunlight and emphasize their builder's skill in stonework and proportion. Lost in unsynchronized history, the precolumbian cultures of Central and South America will one day be recognized as equals, and in many respects as superiors, to their Mediterranean counterparts. *Photo 85, Ruins of Monte Alban, Oaxaca, Mexico, 1983*, presents an acropolis of much greater size than the one in Athens. The scale of the valley is breathtaking, and while the ruins are in a state of confused reconstruction, the original arrangement obviously consisted of a circus. This circuit-shaped space demands a spectacle of colorful and elaborate costumes, massive headdresses and rites as stirring as anything ever held in the Roman Coliseum. To imagine colorful throngs covering the stepped pyramids during a transition of power, or other ceremonials, makes me wonder what comparable spaces we may leave to future generations. They will certainly not be in our capitol city! Archaeologists in the year 5,000 A.D. will not find comparable satisfaction from the ruins that we leave behind.

Photo 86, Rani Pokhari Shrine, Kathmandu, Nepal, 1985, commemorates the love of a mother for her son. Built upon the site of the destroyed temple, this public waterbasin lies in the heart of the city, and its design serves the four necessities of a memorial. It raises your curiosity, makes you want to know why, allows you to appreciate its raison d'etre, and lets you recall its distinctive setting over time, distance, and condition. The mountains on the horizon, the flat reflective quality of the water, the constantly changing backdrop of clouds, and the isolation rendered by the access bridge combine to create a jewel-like setting where brilliant reflections seem to pamper reality.

The backwaters of the Yamuna River and the luxuriating water buffalo bathing in the summer shallows broaden our understanding of the problems faced by Shah Jahan's designer of the Taj Mahal. *Photo 87, Taj Mahal, Agra, Uttar Pradesh, India, 1985*, accepts an uncommon point of view to record this famous building. It depicts an aspect of the place that is opposite to the usual entrance with its grandiose reflecting pools. Here the viewer's interest is focused on the natural condition of the surrounding terrain. To the left rear, the Shah had wanted a matching black mausoleum for himself. Unfortunately, his heirs did not have the same tender affection, or opportunity, and it was not built. We can look at this failure in a number of ways, but I prefer to believe that it was because pairs of things seldom attain greatness. One likeness detracts from the other. Greatness does not come in pairs. The Taj Mahal is situated on a platform that raises it above the surrounding terrain and the realities of Indian poverty. The environment seen here illustrates the social costs of such magnificence and lasting beauty. Beauty and social costs are commonly in conflict with one another. What is the real cost of beauty, or the pain of its lack? Who is to judge the lasting value of a television in every room, or a Taj Mahal?

Photo 88, Giant Stone Buddha, Leshan, Sechuan, China, 1988, and *Photo 89, Access Lookout, Giant Buddha, Leshan, Sechuan, China, 1988*, combine to express scale, access and the statue's relation to the convergence of the Minjiang-Dadu and Quingyi Rivers. The clifflike stone riverbank from which it is carved allows an imposing view of the city of Leshan and the flatland on the other side of the river. Myth has it that the Buddha was carved to subdue the dangerous currents. It required one hundred years to complete. Primary access is by boat, and a series of shrines, carvings, and outlooks occupy a full day's visit. As these photographs indicate, it seems that the Chinese people take a special joy from stairways, outlooks and overviews. Perhaps it is such unusual conditions as this one that provide needed opportunities to escape overcrowding in the cities. The Chinese land-mass appears to the traveler as having been completely reshaped by human hands. The Chinese are prolific diggers and carvers and insatiable changers of the landscape.

Photo 89 illustrates this passion for climbing, carving, and looking. The designers of this Buddha, the largest in the world and over two hundred thirty feet tall, had an uncanny ability to exploit exciting outlooks, as they used the necessary stair landings as viewing platforms as well as to give access to the upper reaches of this colossus. The approach to the Giant Buddha demands that the visitor share the statue's outlook as he climbs, but at landings the visitor's refreshed gaze is reversed. On descending, the opposite sequence of distant and intimate views is required. A religious memorial can have more than one purpose. It can even teach pilgrims to look properly, to see better.

Religious colossi, as memorials, as symbols of unchallenged authority, are used in many religions, but particularly in Buddhism and Christianity. The religions differ in their use of symbols and literal personification of religious figures. Christianity prefers the cross or crucifix as graphic symbols, while Buddhism makes a more uniform use of Buddha, in human form. The many contrasts between this giant stone Buddha and the grandiose figure of the Corvocado Christ rising almost twenty-five hundred feet above Rio de Janiero contrast occidental and oriental preferences. Both seem to seek to awe the beholder, but one exerts authority through overpowering scale and remoteness while the other is more accessible, humane and yet mysterious. The mystery of the Leshan Buddha, seeming to rise out of a muddy and turbulent river, is quite different to the pristine and aloof impersonality of the Corvacado statue of Christ. One is patiently cut from the stone of its natural surroundings and insists that the user recognize the grace of nature while the other is artificially formed and poured, as ersatz stone, seemingly in opposition to nature. The Corvacado statue uses the natural advantages of its location to command respect and, in my mind, force its conception upon the viewer. The Corvocado is overpowering and dominates nature, while the Leshan Buddha was conceived as a more fitting outgrowth of its surround.

Mountains suddenly rearing up from the ocean and great stone escarpments alongside rushing rivers seem likely places to memorialize and express lasting reverence. Flat alluvial soil provides less opportunity and demands greater ingenuity. *Photo 90, Chao Phya River, from Wat Arun, Bangkok, Thailand, 1987*, overlooks one of Bangkok's most popular temple compounds. Almost solely reached by boat, the Temple of the Dawn is of Khmer heritage, and like its many related Thai counterparts, is mysterious to the western visitor. The contorted carvings of the human figure, the zoomorphic embellishments, and the quiet and unassuming deportment of local visitors are coupled with the active mercantile life of the community. An environment of festive temporal pleasures is subtly intermixed with religious memorabilia. There is a vibrant and festive, yet restrained, dignity to a place that brings together a wide range of races and age groups. Steep climbs to lofty outlooks overviewing the noisy river traffic are only separated by a few steps from quiet places for calm meditation.

Death, with its happy and sorrowful memories, touches all of us. Throughout the world the same essential influences are confronted in very different ways, but grief is universal and a normal human reaction is an attempt to recover, or perpetuate, the memory of the person that is gone. Some cultures do this with happy events, such as music and dance, while others adopt morbid practices and seem to revel in emotional pain. Memory and memorials have many faces, but my travels convince me that all human creatures want to leave something on earth that will make the world a better place because of their existence.

The universal human desire to have, and to acknowledge, achievements that go beyond individual material rewards is even more basic than the tenets of formal religion. I am convinced that there is a living force within all of us that clamors to achieve some form of beauty, as an expression of universal love. This common characteristic is exhibited at all levels and in all cultures. The vehicle used can be religious icons, the tools of daily trade, or even the implements of war. Love, pride of accomplishment, beauty, and unusual utility are often combined in these objects of common usage. The attributes of objects much less grandiose than the memorials just described often express the intentions of the maker, and in some cases the culture of the makers, better than larger and more well known relics of the past. Pride of design, craftsmanship, and recognition, whether represented in abstract sculpture, recognized as a special event of nature, or in working tools, such as boats, are worthy of analysis when we consider men's deeper hopes for life. Such objects are concerned with immediate needs, both physical and emotional, rather than merely memorializing events of the past.

XII   SCULPTURE AND BOATS

Sculpture and boats seem to grow from the same emotional responses. A boat, even without ornament or decoration is often pure sculpture, a graceful floating mobile, as anyone viewing a Nordic galley knows. Boats are meant to transport people on water. Sculpture is intended to convey thought and emotion. Beyond such rudimentary functions the separation of these two models of human thought becomes difficult for they serve many of the same human needs. Often combined, sculpture and boats represent the spirit and sense of aliveness of their makers. Each, in their many applications, are symbols of felt but heretofore unrecognized needs. They are emotionally charged shapes that express more than their basic purpose.

Such qualities as curiosity, freedom, and power have been expressed by both boats and sculpture throughout the ages. They have sought help and promised to give it; they have attempted to communicate man's needs to God and god's instructions to man; and they have threatened, and seduced, and promised salvation. As expressions of their designers' subconscious they convey meanings beyond their immediate utility. Sculpture associated with ships and boats has been used to intimidate the enemy, to reassure the crew, and to petition God in a good cause.

Emblematic sculpture has been made part of boats from the masthead to the bowsprit and from the transom frame to the poop deck. During the seventeenth century all functioning parts of ships and their armaments were lavishly carved with nonutilitarian sculpture. Sculptors became so

over zealous, and their handiwork so excessive, that ships actually capsized due to their exuberance. As symbolism outweighed function utility was lost. Much the same thing happened with American automobiles during the 1950's and with the false decoration of buildings under the auspices of Post Modernism. Obviously, the search for symbolic spiritual values can at times overburden conscious reason.

Sculpture is a more general term than carving, since carving is always extractive, while sculpture can be either additive, as with clay, or subtractive, as with stone. Both carving and sculpture are at least thirty-five thousand years old and together they record human development through a chain of implements, containers, and more recently, vehicles. Long before the written word, traditions were communicated through stone carvings and clay tablets. Bronze, a mixture of copper and tin that resists exposure to weather better than even stone was cast in China over two thousand years ago. A description of the process was written over a thousand years ago. These epoch altering discoveries have, like the printing press, allowed exchanges between minds separated by hundreds or even thousands of years.

It is much more difficult to be glib with sculpture than with the written word. This may be why sculptors and writers are so different; however, many of their essential functions are the same. They both seek to communicate through time and both require introspection and thought prior to action. They record ideas through succeeding generations; register the orthodoxies of their time; and expose the chronology of traditions handed down from generation to generation. Sculpture is a record of thought, always involving a message to the future that evokes emotions, the human spirit, and a sense of beauty.

Sculpture made by the amateur, the novice, often displays significant intuitive perceptions. Usually based upon some actual belief or physical need, the vernacular sculptor whether boat builder or decorator of a loved person's sepulcher, creates shapes that have a clarity of purpose that is rare to find in the work of designers removed from direct emotional involvement. The traditional builder's way of thinking and feeling, whether of boat or sculpture, is rooted in a past that balances attitudes, customs and taste. When they depart from traditional methods it is never for whimsy alone. The shapes and profiles of their handiwork evolve slowly through trial and error; using and feeling, not so much for aesthetic purity as to meet real needs.

Through time and use a sense of possession can take hold, whether from a decorative sculpture or the handling qualities of a boat. They can both assume anthropomorphic qualities as they come to represent human responses. Boats can develop almost human personalities that satisfy their owner's emotional needs. Perhaps this is why boats carry female names.

Boats, beyond the purity of their profiles, often have sculpture incorporated into their utilitarian parts. Their shapes often reflect place, time, and use, as well as a conforming sense of beauty. Boats can exude trust, love, power, and protection. They extend man's understanding of nature and they have the seemingly human capacity to act well or badly. Of course, as we judge boats we judge their owners and their uses. Boats are often their owners' created talismen with the traits of the owner clearly evident. While boats may serve a psychological life of their own, they must also perform utilitarian functions. This is their essence.

Boats do more than satisfy the emotions and ego of their owner. Sculpture, on the other hand, does not require physical utility beyond having qualities that are cerebrally and tactily satisfying. Both boats and sculpture should excite something within the viewer's mind that vitalizes and brings about sensual satisfaction. I cannot imagine good sculpture that I do not want to touch, or a good boat that I do not want to feel under way. Who can really appreciate Brancusi's *Bird in Space* and not want to feel it?

Photo 91, Gilded Malla King, Durbar Square, Baktapur, Nepal, 1985, is a jewel-like public image of a gilded Nepalese ruler as he kneels, gazing down to the public square below. Animated by dark shadows and darker birds perched intimately on his rounded anatomy and smiling face the monument bears none of the unctuous formality of western officialdom. The naga, or seven-headed serpent, rising above the king, and a favorite perch for the Buddhist birds, is a mythical symbol of superhuman qualities.

In comparison with most European sculptures the smiling and obsequious likeness of a thoughtful and seemingly compliant king is quite different to the less stylized but more threatening occidental counterparts. The capital, supported by a tall shaft, consists of the symbolic lotus flower whose mass emphasizes the figure above.

The Malla king, kneeling alone in a public square, atop an isolated shaft requires a very different perspective and presence to the receding rectangles of *Photo 92, Khmer Ruins, Prasat Phnom Rung, Pimai, Thailand, 1987.* This elongated passageway joins a series of temples and requires the viewer to focus down a gun barrel with a series of lateral surprises. The visitor's attention is held to a distant climax, but in the interim, the eye is enticed by crossing shadows, deeply textured carvings, and spatial variations. The Malla king unfolds as you visually circumnavigate its presence while the Khmer Ruins demand the same unshakeable concentration as you walk straight ahead to sense the scene as it unfolds around the viewer in another way.

The movement of the viewer is extremely important in seeing and sensing sculpture properly. There is no single point of view as there is in some two dimensional paintings. Sculpture requires a dynamic viewer and it should be the sculptor's intention to lead the viewer onward with subtlety and inference. In *Photo 93, Seven Headed Naga, Phra Buddha Band, Saraburi to Lopburi, Thailand, 1987,* we see the hooded profile of a bronze abstraction of the seven mythological heads that by custom sits

atop its coiled body. More like a traditional Chinese dragon, the body of the naga writhes and twists its sensuous way up the center of a stairway. The worshippers going to the shrines above are guided by the polished bronze body as they ascend. The tactile quality of this directional sculpture is made obvious as the visitor's hands continuously polish the surface of the bright metal.

The moving eye is again a participant in the linear passage shown in *Photo 94, Stone Forest, near Kunming, Yunnan, China, 1988.* The voluptuous and intertwining bulges and tuberous shapes left by thousands of years of water passage anticipates the polished stone sculptures of Sir Henry Moore. Here nature has used colors, shapes, and variations of light to create a complex work of art. Human movement is not an essential part of the composition but there is a sense that it once existed even if only as the recomposed entrails of a giant, perhaps of the Leshan Buddha!

Mythology, humor, and sheer deference can create sculpture of great richness. *Photo 95, Roof Finials, Durbar Square, Baktapur, Nepal, 1988,* shows how the sky can meet a building with interest and bemusement. A mythical animal, seemingly a turtle but with elongated neck and legs, attracts nesting birds while musical finials reach toward the sky and a golden medallion hangs from a pendant. What exists within this veiled rooftop sanctum? What strange apparition gazes outward to appraise our approach? A culture that cares for its visitor with such subtlety and finesse as to have windbells, lavishly carved brackets, and a roof built more like jewelry than a building represents a rare sensibility. It is near here that the Chineses pagoda with its stacked roofs originated, and it must be a similar love of subtle profile that now leads our discussion to boats and their refined sculptural shapes.

The bright yellow boat shown in *Photo 96, Wooden Longboat, Salvador-Bahia, Brazil, 1977,* is typical of vernacular constructions that express essential needs everywhere on earth. In the tropics much commerce is dependent upon water travel. This primitive dugout, in its updated construction, stretches its length to direct the eye to the activities of a fish market. The refined shapes of these very slender craft have reached near classic proportions in much the same way as *Photo 97, Work Boats on Rio Negro, Manaus, Brazil, 1977.* This photograph depicts the standard Amazon River boats of today. The sizes and number of decks vary widely but the shapes, materials, and shading devices have become classically similar. These boats are even more standardized than the houses in the background, yet they state in unequivocal terms that their owners would like to be as different as possible.

Character in boats is not always easily recognized or described. In *Photo 98, Vernacular Boat, Ujung Pandang, Sulawesi, Indonesia, 1987,* the physiognomy of a graceless little harbor boat brings forth a chuckle until we notice some of its carefully conceived parts. It is not only the cheerful red highlights, but the arrangements of the bowsprit and jib, the tripartite mast and loading boom support, the dual outboard rudders and many other personal innovations that should convince any onlooker that here is a thoughtful and innovative person. The sail may be conventional but a creative mind can be seen in all of the boat's details. Judging from this picture alone, is it any wonder that the Japanese thought to place sawmills on their timber ships plying between the West Coast and Japan?

Photo 99, Nile River Boats, Luxor, Egypt, 1980, is typical of conditions in many parts of the world. Here at least ten boats, apparently of separate ownerships, are almost identically built, painted, and rigged, even to the gangplanks. Underway and with full sail these are beautiful and almost lifelike creatures as they glide against the current, but how can their owners have reached such a state of complete acceptance and standardization? Freedom of thought and initiative are always expressed in differences, not in such glaring similarities. When variations do not exist, as with taxi cabs, some form of repression must exist. Even Henry Ford should wince at such conformity. Enough can be too much.

Sculptural shapes are all about us and influence our lives. Boats are but one example. As we walk around something, see it from various positions and receive pleasurable responses, whether it is a member of the opposite sex, an animal, a mountain, or an automobile, it has sculptural qualities.

Much of the physical world is revealed through our perception of motion and movement. The shape of a boat tells us how it will handle; the position of a sculpted head can reveal anguish or ecstacy. But, we do not yet understand how we perceive motion. It is certainly not as simple as Edison's sequence of photographic frames for we cannot explain how our minds fill-in the gaps between the frames so that we perceive smooth movement rather than jerky jumps. When neurobiologists finally unravel this mystery it will undoubtedly allow a great leap forward in our ability to control visual perceptions and let us expand our comprehension of sculptural assemblies. Painting and still photography must now be stored and reproduced in two dimensions and sculptural holograms do not allow a sense of reality as we walk around them. When stereoscopic motion lets us sense three dimensions with reality a new frontier will allow creative opportunities for active minds; however, the age-old communication between the individual mind and rock-solid sculptural shapes will remain as powerful and influential as ever. Computers can create a general sense of volumes and movement but only in a limited way. Compare a walk through a sculpture garden with its computer image.

We now live in many types of housing located on a great variety of sites, yet every home should have its own distinct character, shape, and outlook. The quality of the unit varies with the capacities of the individual and the traditions of the place. A miracle buried within each of us relates material and spiritual values and creates tastes and appetites that are handed from parent to child. Yet enormous similarities in

psychological responses exist between peoples around the world. A comparison of some existing living conditions will let us better understand our individual priorities and help us weigh our own tastes.

XIII HOMES AND HOUSING

Flying over the United States, the visitor must be struck by the drabness of our cities and their suburbs. Composed of repetitive subdivisions laid out in regulated grids or monotonous curves, the standardized homes of North Americans are indeed homely. These urban habitats, viewed from above, give the impression of regimented, stamped-out, repetitive cells.

Such thoughts must occur to frequent fliers and influence their judgment. We all realize that what we euphemistically call homes are really no more than housing, but we do not improve these conditions. A system has assumed control. The surveyor's, realtor's, and lawyer's convenience, the right angle, designs based solely upon the advantages of selling and speculation, the economies of repetitive mass production and limited life, and the controls demanded by a homogenized government control our housing. The family and its individual values, has given way to purely numerical measure. "One man, one vote" has required the acceptance of "head counts." We live in standardized and sanitized conditions that are little different from those used in the design and construction of breeding barns for animals.

As we travel abroad and recognize the superior living conditions and greater daily satisfactions of other cultures many of us wonder how we came to our present condition. It is becoming more and more evident that the automobile has been misused and now literally dictates our daily existence and economic stability. Our homes and family life have been deformed through the misuse of the family car. As a nation we are shackled to mislocated housing and inefficient travel patterns.

A vast difference exists between a home and a house. A house is a place to hide, a structure for human habitation. In comparison, a home defines a place to dwell securely and happily. The home is the basic building block of society, a place where we are supposedly secure and supreme. Home is where we can be sure that we properly belong. It is the most personal, intimate, and qualitative of our environments. Our homes provide refuge, rest, and emotional reassurances. The family home should be tailored to their idiosyncracies. Home is where the heart is, where we can create our very own utopia.

The essential difference between house and home is never its cost or size, but is always its spirit. Whether a traveler in a strange land or an archaeologist attempting to understand a bygone culture, we all judge people through their physical surroundings. Today, one of the most revealing aspects of any culture is its housing or collections of homes. Through finite works we can interpret the hopes and dreams of entire communities.

Photo 100, Island of Thira (Santorini), Sea of Crete, Greece, 1980, a volcanic island that has suffered an explosive history but now exhibits a tranquil existence all its own. Settled two and half millenia ago by forbears of the Phoenicians, it has been free of natural catastrophes for the last hundred years. Idiosyncratic buildings cling to the slope through the use of interlocking terraces, secret passages, and retaining walls. The unusual array of visual outlooks is not disturbed by modern vehicles so the horizon and quiet overview are available to everyone. Built of local materials and representing a long heritage of consistent social values the variety of physical shapes is consolidated by the importance of distant views. A collective sense of unity is expressed through a single monochromatic finish on the plastic shapes of the homes and churches. The variety of shades and shadows produced as the sun moves through the day is in extreme contrast to the glass sheathed apartments of our cities. Here there is no need to reflect what is already seen for there is something even more attractive around the next corner. The outlook excites the spirit within every onlooker, whether visitor or resident. This is a place that revels in its isolation, independence and idiosyncratic adaptation of beautiful shapes.

A less deamatic location, *Photo 101, Seaside Homes, Cape Point to Capetown, Republic of South Africa, 1981*, obviously does not contain the same historic and cultural forerunners. The striated stone formations in the background push seaward as they erode into the Atlantic Ocean. Nestled between giant boulders, a seaside community of European origin has adapted to a dramatic new location. Lush planting has been given a rocky foothold as the wealthy occupants look away from the relations to their rear. Vehicular access exists but is has not been allowed to dominate the more important visual potential of the place.

This more recent development is in strange contrast to a much older and more secure culture. *Photo 102, Neckar River Homes, from Heidelberg Castle, West Germany, 1984*, depicts one of the more intellectually stable and contributive societies on earth. The purposeful joy of the place seems justified by it many contributions to the growth of European thought. The center of German Calvanism, Heidelberg's spirit of inquiry puts it at the head of any hierarchal chain of educational communities. It was here, six hundred years ago, that universities began. Along with beer hall antics and student duels of honor they created one of the world's greatest scholarly communities. The calm good grooming of the large but not ostentatious homes, within an idealic scene, reflects the families of thoughtful individuals who have resided here for centuries. These are not the homes of robber barons along the banks of the Hudson River. These homes represent rewards earned through important contributions

to man's knowledge of himself. The materials of construction and the shapes of the buildings themselves seem to exude stability. While the homes may have many traditional similarities they are all slightly different and express the distinct values of individuals.

In a completely different cultural tradition, *Photo 103, Hillside Housing, Guanajuato, Mexico, 1989*, is of a planned community for Mexican workers. Standard structures are repeated in varying combinations as the housing project envelops the hillside. For the Mexican-Indians who are always so expressive in their aesthetic efforts this barren expression of stateism must be truly unacceptable and may therefore soon become just another barrio. It will then have flowers and other amenities that better express the deeper sensitivities of its occupants. Such housing can become homes, even when conceived as mass developments like this, but to do this they must provide more than refuge and rest. A home must lay hold of the occupant's affections and be the place where they find real satisfaction and emotional revival.

Before air conditioning most people seemed to seek an outlook, or view, as a primary component of acceptable homesites. For this reason building sites, from the hill towns of Italy to the slopes of Peru, have elicited a sense of visual delight. Both thermal comfort and visual uplift are available to the residents of *Photo 104, Mountain Ridge Houses, Darjeeling, West Bengal, India, 1985*. Located over seven thousand feet above sea level and only forty miles south of Mt. Everest, this old English hill station gave these sojourners periodic relief from their sweltering assignments to the south. Dwellings flow down the steep sides of a ridge that overlooks the Himalayan foothills on one side and Mt. Kanchenjunga on the other. From the early nineteenth century the English shared the ridge with merchants while permanent residents clambered down percipitous paths and steps to their eagle's nest overviews. Unlike *Photo 103* where clouds float above, here, they may be either above or below and are often intimate associates of the observers. This and the altitude causes the quality of light to make rapid and erratic changes that enhance the euphoria so natural to the place.

The original subdivision of land in Darjeeling was not made by the dull conformities of surveyors but by the necessity of sound footing. The repetition so much a part of mercantile man and his two dimensional speculative plots is not applicable here. The difficulties of access and available construction methods required a randomness that better satisfies the human spirit. Flowing down the ridge between gullies, the houses are located as naturally as if deposited by the flow of melting snow. Limited access creates an environment where buildings convey the visual sense of what men can carry on their backs while their feet seek to grip the steep slopes. A very human scale is combined with incomparable overviews, to create picturesque building opportunities that remain vivid in human memory. Individual differences are given free reign and the identity of self expression. Compare, if you will, the visual opportunities available here and those from the fiftieth floor of an apartment in Manhattan. Which represents the real social hiatus?

Building on a slope has the advantage of two opposing design opportunities. Looking outward from the slope, the view seems to stretch on forever, a visual macrocosm. Looking backward toward the slope, and dug into the side of it, a small garden allows detailed contemplation of the more intimate aspects of life, a visual microcosm. One view demands a telescope and the other a magnifying glass. Living between the infinite, without, and the infinite, within, such a house balances the extremes of all physical outlooks. Here the views can be constantly related. The potential of the distant horizon and the up-close detail of the courtyard constitute a major advantage for the steeply sloping site. Living in such a place becomes more than a passive experience. It allows dynamic comparison to become everyday events.

The single family house and the multifamily complex have long histories. Their traditions spring from different needs. One has rural roots while the other apparently developed to accommodate urban needs. *Photo 105, Main Court, Group G, Tikal Ruins, Guatemala, 1987* is an example of early multiple or row housing. Situated near the center of a great ceremonial center, the specifics of the occupant's way of life are not known but the units surround large courtyards that seem to anticipate developments that are in use today. The design represents a humane and advanced urban life style that is much like our own. Every viewer should make their own interpretation of such scenes as they analyze the riddles of such archaeological remains.

Photo 106, Private Houses, Wanshai, Hong Kong, 1983 and *Photo 107, Public Housing, Wanshai, Hong Kong, 1983*, were taken seconds apart and from the same location through a telephoto lens. *Photo 106* shows conditions that the Hong Kong authorities were destroying and replacing with the tower housing shown in *Photo 107*. Such well meaning efforts to create better organized, more safe and sanitary, more accountable housing seem to be universal in the world's great urban centers, in New York, in Moscow, everywhere. But, is this really better? A contrast between physical survival and emotional survival, the survival of the human spirit, is clearly evident in these two pictures.

In *Photo 106*, the residents are closely associated with plants, the seasons, a variety of opportunities for physical self-improvement and personally conceived improvisations and private control. They can hear the rain on their roofs and see it cascade from the eaves. They can have secret places, nooks and crannies; they can be individuals and accommodate whims. In *Photo 107*, they do not have these things. The residents have become captives of a system wherein all of their physical needs are safely and sanitarily provided for, like white mice in a laboratory. They are forced to respond as automatons to the same kinky orders. In these

towers of predetermined responses the occupants have been isolated from nature and the seasons and such primeval needs as hearing rain, associating with growing plants, and being permitted an occasional nonconforming whim. They have become eggs in an incubator run by anonymous and sovereign authorities. They are now countable and accountable, to everyone but themselves.

The wild excesses of the savage have been replaced by the cultivated consensus of the termite colony. Life may be longer and less contorted, but where are the vital satisfactions, the rewards for risks taken, the sense of self-esteem, self-determination, and hope. Man may not be an island, and while we obviously cannot exist completely alone we must demand the rights of reasonable self-sufficiency, instead of being forced to accept the concept of living by the lowest common denominator on a life-long, social, heart-lung machine. The cost of individual decisions, of occupying our own home instead of society's housing, is substantial. Such freedom demands physical effort and financial risk but it seems to me that this is a small price to pay for our emotional and spiritual freedom.

The family home in an agrarian setting is shaped by the necessities of the growing seasons and demands of the fields themselves. The building shapes derived from these needs are slowly transferred from rural locations, to villages, to cities, but many of the original shaping forces remain. The necessity for intimate human relations with plants and growing things is as evident in today's suburban houses and multistory apartments as it was in the beginning. *Photo 108, Valley Farms, Paro to Thimphu, Bhutan, 1989*, illustrates the tradition-driven shape of a medieval culture as it still exists. Toil and the habits of manual labor produce a seemingly romantic and pleasant agrarian farmstead, until we look more closely. There are no flowers here and mud and weeds surround the yards and entryways, as we realize that mud stubbornly seeps and sticks between the toes of the bare feet of the residents. Such crude encampments may be seen as a part of a secure life, but they also record a life with little joie de vivre. They are places to hide at night, to survive. They are interesting to see from a distance, to photograph, but not to live in. They have at times been idealized in literature but they are really no more than open-air sweat shops, places of interminable toil, where the necessities of nature demand that the welfare of plants dominate man's spirit.

A viewer with a resourceful mind should pose questions to himself that exploit the fuller meaning of any photograph. This cannot be done passively. To fully explore the photographic image, all answers lead to another level of self analysis. The photograph is no more than a catalyst for priming new visual insights. The basis of all seeing is founded in what we knew before we looked. The measure of what we saw is what we are able to bring to our next visual confrontation.

The discussion here, along with the photographs, should serve as opportunities for the reader, the viewer, to apply their experiences to what is said here. Hopefully, the reader will become more conscious of the differences between homes and houses, family values and individual needs.

As discussed earlier, individual, families and their values are grouped and averaged in our minds to create communities and governments. These, in turn generate their own character and visual metaphors. We often judge entire cultures through our personal interpretations of their collective dwellings, much as we do wasps, by the size and shape of their nests. Such physical generalizations may be wrong but it is how our minds have been schooled to operate. The profile of a building such as the Parthenon or the Taj Mahal can symbolize our feelings toward an entire culture. In the inverse, every photographic image of such common items as buildings, that involves our analytical processes, usually begins with our interpretation of the culture, the society, that brought it into being. Our minds follow precedents that are learned.

Each of the photographs discussed here raised questions in my mind, not simply regarding homes and housing, but about light, reality, and life in general. The assignment to homes and housing came much after I selected them from hundreds of similar images. Some mystery within each attracted my attention. I will never be completely sure of what it was that I saw.

Governments attempt to bring order to the lives of individuals, families, communities, and entire cultures. The symbols that they leave in the function, shape and location of their constructed icons are fascinating. They can represent many aspects of life and its manifold conditions. We can all judge ourselves by what we see, what interests us most in these images of implied authority and power. The central mystery is still the same, why we like what we like.

We seldom take time to consider the many symbolisms that lie just below our conscious thought. Like dreams that may only represent the static of idle brain transmissions, our minds must be constantly directed toward reasonable goals. The range of questions that our inquiring eyes pose as we scan the following photographs can be reduced to categories but they are never adequate.

XIV POWER AND PUBLIC PLACES

Power is a captivating term, something we all seek for ourselves but hope to avoid in others. Power has magnetic appeal but it can become repugnant when we observe its uses. The fascination that we feel when we see the marks of power, particularly built symbols meant to impress and dominate their onlookers, is difficult to describe. How can we sort-out why some men seek to exhibit their control over others; for power in its most elemental state means that one person is able to control, to overpower, others.

The symbols of personal power that men leave behind are based upon their control of other men. Their ultimate power, during life, was often based upon their capacity to create fear and destruction. Mortals can have no greater authority than the power of life or death over their contemporaries. Historically the power of mortal men was based upon their destructive potential, while the ultimate power of gods was their creative force coupled with promises of salvation. The power of men is always now and must be proven. The power of gods is in the past, or the future, and need simply be believed.

As I review images of constructions resulting from physical expressions of power, I try to imagine conditions at the time when they were built. Their external physiques can only be appraised through an understanding of the opinions of their contemporaries and the beliefs prevailing in their own time. In this regard I have often tried to understand why I like high places, why I prefer being at the top of a hill to being in the valley, why I like the upper floors of a hotel or office building. The explanation may not be as complex as I once thought and may simply be based upon gravity and a primitive concern for the best and most defensible position in combat.

Accepting the proposition that the most compelling force on earth is the power of life or death over our peers, height becomes very important. Before the introduction of explosives combat was largely measured in animal strength. Few mechanical devices were available for hand-to-hand combat; however, men soon learned that the advantages of gravity could be decisive. Pushing, rolling, or throwing downward has the great advantage of additional speed and impact over throwing upward. The symbolism of being "on top of a thing" was then certainly more than illusory. The best defensive positions allowed the defenders to look down and to throw down upon their adversaries. Gravity, the advantage of height, could determine victory in combat. The lesson lies deeply buried within our primordial consciousness. Basketball coaches understand!

Before the advent of explosives, social and governmental units were usually limited to small nations or city states ruled by theocrats. Leadership was near at hand and individual interpretations of events were based upon direct observations. The ultimate power of the state was usually composed of an aristocracy that combined unchallenged power along with a sense of responsibility, whether exercised by a tyrant or a benevolent overlord. Throughout the world there were many units of government where ultimate power resided within an individual whose only limit of authority was the spirit world of religion. Conflict was constant and height was recognized as important to victory and was therefore a constant concern of the warrior class. Redoubts and strongholds became essential physical and psychological assets. Height and access to drinking water, seeming opposites, were the treasures of combative leadership. The possession of high ground with life sustaining water provided many medieval victories and may have been one of the primary reasons for the beginning of royal tenure. Height, outlook, overview, must trace some of their current importance to such ancient, if not hereditary, subconscious feelings. The term "gravity of the situation" may stem from such primitive associations. During the thousands of years before man obtained explosives, his height, relative to his opponent, could be decisive in life or death struggles. Such beliefs understandably spilled-over into his religious beliefs. Heaven was thought of as being above and hell below, and then we created the heavenly redoubt. Such ranging, even ridiculous assumptions can give new dimensions to creative possibilities as we select from among the many options available in a visual determination.

The fourteenth century literally burst upon western man as explosives were introduced from China. Old ways and values could no longer be maintained. Leadership became less physical and direct, more impersonal and cerebral. Information grew in such leaps that it often rested in groups rather than individuals and was distributed by indirect, mass means. Countries became larger, colonialism evolved and grew into great opposing philosophical and religious ideologies. Plutocracies attained ultimate power as their internal, but sometimes international and mercantile oligarchies dominated both the underclass and the patrician. One man, one vote, came to be manipulated by the economic forces that supplanted formal religion. By mid twentieth century the fear of chemical explosives eliminated all forms of serious personal combat. The transition from gunpowder to hydrogen and binary chemical bombs had reduced opposing units of world government to three or four. The potential combatant's necessity of holding the high ground moved on to controlling access to energy sources and raw materials. The earlier transcendent importance of religion lost its potential to concerns for ethnic equality and democratic method. Redoubts were still built, inside the center of mountain fastnesses, but they became very expensive and apparently quite vulnerable.

As we consider photographs representing these two vastly different epochs of human evolution, what were the issues of most lasting significance? How can we celebrate the winning of the ball game until we know the final score? How can we judge the past without at least a brief estimate of what we believe is yet to come? What will follow the twentieth century? Will the very judgments that we are now making have unfortunate later effects? This question represents the metaphysical center of each of our personal searches for truth, even the understanding of photographs.

It seems to me that real leadership is becoming very remote from the people. Government has become a quasi specialized vocation that is removed from the governed and is largely figurative. Our elected leaders more and more accept the views of a world-spanning news network that is insidious, increasingly inbred, socially biased, and is seeking an ultimate authority. The news industry now sees itself as sacrosanct, invincible,

and unerring. Political leadership grows more diffuse, while the power of anonymous minority groups is blandly accepted by the masses as they promise instantaneous, automatic, and democratic determinations by simply allowing the electorate to push buttons as they sit before impersonal television screens. Democratic mobocracy and uncontrolled mercantile pursuits are vulgarizing our few remaining aristocratic qualities. The only significant measure of human accomplishment must now be expressed in financial terms. The pursuit of riches is the only game in town and yet there is little of real value to buy. In warfare it seems quite likely that all explosives may have become passe. The control of chemoelectrical brain functions of entire societies may now be possible by either television diffusion or the use of VCR magnetic fields. Aldus Huxley's *Brave New World* and George Orwell's *1984* may come to pass without war, or physical discomfort. Our future flower wars, unlike those held centuries ago in Central America to obtain sacrificial victims, will not take prisoners, only units of economic control. Economic theory will become classically organized and spread as evenly over mankind as hot butter on toast. Any concern for the human spirit, the will to become greater than we are scheduled to be, will become more and more implausible. The irrationality of physical or emotional redoubts on earth will be generally accepted. Even the old escape into the home will be dispensed with and we will all depart this earth with our number inscribed upon impersonal metal cannisters, containing our ashes, that are placed in timeless orbit about the earth. This third epoch, unlike the five thousand years of the first, or the six hundred years of the second, may last until we realize the warmth of the next ice age.

As we gird our loins for this period of growing benevolence, we should examine the views of our predecessors as revealed through their executed works and public places. Perhaps a careful reading of their hopes and intentions will leave more than their ashes in our mouths. It is even possible that we will perceive truths that have greater significance than simply relating our spiritual values to combat.

This rather depressing preface is intended to act as a catalyst to actuate a searching analysis of the following nine photographs. Hopefully your interpretation of the values expressed within, and supposedly by, the physical remains of societies, political systems, and technological capacities will allow you to envision, and participate in, the development of a better world. Each picture, the objects shown, and the conditions of man, then and now, conveys a challenge to both interpretation and future action. The histories of social, political, and physical sciences do not promise that we will ultimately find pure truth as an isolated entity. They do assure us that major change will develop from individual minds who find their inspirations in unusual places.

Photo 109, Rhine Castle, Rudesheim to St. Goarshaven, West Germany, 1984, illustrates a continuous development from medieval times to the present. The German personality that shares the importance of heraldry and homes, with all of its contradictions, is clearly expressed. Rhine River castles have always shared the benevolence of the waters for drink, travel, defense, and spiritual revival. Here a redoubt is built high up a natural defensive ridge but not so high as to not have access to water. Generations of toil are revealed in the retaining walls and the ominous presence of the battlements that look out on them. Who conceived of this arrangement? What unrevealed affairs have been consummated here? Why have the physical remains lasted? What are the political, social, and scientific changes that have occurred to let it still stand as if it were a symbolic cadaver twisting in the wind? The decorative demands of powerful leaders often combine a token of esteem for their subjects with an administrative expression of their power, invulnerability, and immortality.

Photo 100, Tusha Hiti Royal Bath, Durbar Square, Patan, Nepal, 1985, depicts a ceremonial environment that remains impressive for its icons and many other reflections of power, a way of life reserved for omnipotent rulers. *Photo 111, Domes Over Main Gate, Fatehpur Si-Kri, near Agra, India, 1985,* contains over thirty dome-shaped pavilions atop the ceremonial gateway to the city. Built as a new capitol of the Moghul Empire by Emperor Akbar, it was occupied for only a few years when its water sources proved inadequate. Rich in color, the significance of the shapes was cause for their reuse when a new capitol of India was built in the twentieth century. Power can be symbolized through such details.

Height, simple but overwhelming, is often used to dominate a place. *Photo 112, Tuomiokirkko Domkyrkan Cathedral, Helsinki, Finland, 1986,* does just this. Overlooking a busy harborfront, the profile of this oversized ceremonial structure dominates the skyline and its surround. As it rises above the activities of the wharves below a presence that once represented the transcendent power of the church now merely anchors a more secular scene. A pristine view of water, land, and sky presents a picture of ordered natural relations. Even the clouds appear to be in a lock-step of rigorous order.

The defense of faith has many precedents but no better symbol than *Photo 113, Detail, Potala Palace, Lhasa, Tibet, 1988,* the traditional home of the Dali Lama. Located on a rocky outcropping surrounded by higher ranges of the Himalayas the Yellow Hat order of Lamaist monks combined a religious and a quasi military administrative center. Until the 1959 invasion of the Chinese communists this sanctum sanctorum of Lamaism was held to be inviolate. As a beautiful anachronism the stepped defensive retaining walls of the Potala now only represent the remnants of a very old and tenacious faith.

Tibet, long one of mankind's most remote cultures, tried to remain aloof from the problems of the rest of the world. To do this they erected defensive positions in high and beautiful places. *Photo 114, Fort at Gyantze, Tibet, 1988,* joined with a monastery to serve as an outpost of Lamaism. It was not destroyed when finally stormed by the British but was later badly damaged during the Chinese occupation of 1959. Much like precolumbian ruins in Mexico and the Acropolis in Athens, the Dzong, built over six hundred years ago, is surrounded by the fertile land of the Tibetan high plateau. As this great ghost clings to the crest of the hill in the center of a valley, its defensive purpose no longer viable, it has outlived its original purpose except in the imagination of the viewer.

Photo 115, Redoubt near Zhannang, Tibet, 1988, unlike *Photo 114,* is another outgrowth of Tibet's feudal past. Here an overlord built a fortified retreat overlooking the rich valley below. Located atop a ridge at the foot of a mountain, it could easily be identified as being in Europe, except for the shape of the roof on the tower. The structure dominates its vicinity and would certainly have struck awe into those working in the fields below. Such symbols of power have been used to dominate lesser men throughout the ages. This is a lonely sentinel of an age and ego long departed.

Burial traditions that are foreign to our own are always memorable. *Photo 116, Burial Center on Irrawaddy River, Pagan, Burma, 1987,* is a most extraordinary place. For miles in every direction there are great Buddhist memorials. Erected on a plain that now has cultivated rice fields between the monuments, there are hundreds of large and ornate masonry pagodas and temples. This capitol of Ahawratha Buddhism, "the city of a thousand temples," is almost a thousand years of age. Climbing to the top of a temple you can see similar constructions to the very horizon. Few cultures have achieved an equivalent mass of religious or funereal reminders. Quantitatively, even the Egyptian pharaohs could not match the mass of structures honoring the dead. No nation can surpass Burma in the fervor that its people had for building religious tributes to the dead.

Another philosophy of life and leadership is exhibited in *Photo 117, Public Fountain, Patan, Nepal, 1985,* where ornate public fountains with striking cast bronze figures serve the public's daily convenience. Like many such communal water sources, a spirit of cooperative good will pervades the place. The sovereign power is here benevolent and kind. Ages mix on equal terms and life is happy.

There are essential differences between ruling and governing, even though both have access to power. To rule connotes a controlling power and the authority to determine basic policy. To govern does not include the sovereign power and the making of basic policy, but limits its authority to the carrying-out of policy determined earlier. It is for the reader to decide the type of government under which the foregoing public facilities were erected.

The reader should look backward to further analyze personal responses to the photographs just discussed. Do some of the terms listed below cause new images and ideas to well-up? These pictures represent demonstrations of power in public places. How do you respond to the thoughts: that fear underlies all power; that power utilizes force to achieve its ends; that force is essential to all authority; that authority requires acceptance; that acceptance eventually brings about reverence; that reverence seeks the reinforcement of beauty; that beauty generates docility; that docility almost always assures obedience; that obedience is justified by superior beings and controlled by fear; and therefore fear is the basis for all forms of government. Does this make anarchy our only option or determine how we play word games with pictures, or is this only the contortion of an infirm thought?

Without explanations given in religious mythology man's purpose on earth remains unclear. We are told that we cannot live for appetites alone. But, what appetites? Are all of our efforts meaningless unless justified by the tenets of formal religion? I think not.

Let us look at three brief images cast by two cultures removed from each other by five thousand years. One built stone temples to their gods to last through the ages. The other is building towers of trade and commerce designed for a limited life that need only exceed the limits set by fickle financial depreciations. Which practice most nearly serves man's evolving needs?

XV PAST AND PRESENT

Without knowledge of time there is only now, now and its animal instincts. The most important comprehension of man on earth was the remote and anonymous inspiration by someone at the edge of our past who asked: "What should I call the interval between two successive events or acts, whether they be days, tides, or sunrises?" It was in this way that measure must have started. The active recognition of time set man above all other beings and this most essential of perceptions has allowed us to utilize memory, experience, history, and science. Units of the past can be projected into the future. We have also come to understand that it is not only what we do that is important, but when we do it. The greatest challenge that we have within time, is doing, doing something that will influence the future and that time will not totally erase, such as the original perception of time itself. The challenge is eternal. If there is an afterlife with worldly memories the originator of time must be gloating: "now if I had not lived time would not exist and man would still be an animal, because of time I am the inventor of mankind!"

Time is really all that any of us have on earth and it should not be aimlessly wasted. But what is waste? What is productive value? Value in some societies, in some men, in some epochs, is waste in others. Consistency is based upon time and predictable change in our cultural interpretation of value or waste. We need something to measure them by, something physical, that can assemble the subtleties of human thought into things more enduring than words. Words and their etymological interpretations, moving from language to language and time to time, have great importance but as the millenia pass, as time proceeds with its infinite duration, change is inevitable. Objects do not change as fast as the meaning of words used in discussing them. Interpretations of objects change, even as the objects themselves must ultimately vanish, but until they do the objects of human intention reveal our character and hopes more accurately, more succinctly, than their descriptions. Objects and buildings are messages from the past and to the future and as we value and learn from photographic images of these things we will better understand the intentions of their makers. Descriptions of the works of Phidias, the Greek sculptor, are of great importance in helping us to understand the time when they were written, but without analyzing the actual objects of his handiwork such as his frieze on the Parthenon, we are measuring smoke rather than the reality of the fire below.

It is in this sense that we should try to understand cities and their component buildings, but always in regard to their own time. Anyone can measure and rebuild the Parthenon today but twenty-five hundred years ago the challenges were quite different. The selection of the building site was based upon needs that can still be related to similar conditions in other parts of the world both before and after the Parthenon's construction. Speaking in current terms, how would you depict a Periclean contemporary describing the Acropolis in Athens? What aspects of the site or social order would you give priority? What were the values of the Parthenon's designers? What was the building's original measure?

It is the same with our contemporary cities. What are the most relevant values of our time? How are we different from our predecessors and what directions will our accomplishments give to later generations? Will our time be known for space exploration, trade, and distribution of goods, packaging, and production, or the rule of "one man, one vote?" Are these the body building nutrients for a worldwide body politic, or are they mere icings on time tarts? Can such factors be read from the remains of our contemporary cities? Are photographs a means of recording such things? I believe that they can be.

In the same way that positive forces are evident in our society, so are many negative beliefs. The restraint of human progress can be read through such distortions of reason, usually justified on economic grounds, as the "annual model," the intentional manufacture of things with a limited life, for profit alone. The excesses within the legal system, such as those widely practiced by plaintiffs' lawyers where any design innovation is a proper subject for manipulation and extortion through control of the courts, are regressive and wrong.

The current misuse of the word materialism, denegrating the material substance of man's handiwork, rewards the administrator or commentator at the expense of the designer and producer. The producer of better goods and services is seldom rewarded on the same basis as the promoter and the merchandiser, while political power is becoming more and more diffuse and invisibly imbedded within every human creation. Innovation has literally become punishable, while we allow such gross misrepresentations as misleading packaging to be freely passed on to the public. Such perfidious falsity deforms what should be our most cherished potential. Accidental verbal abuse remains unlawful, while willful production of obsolete designs is seldom challenged. Change, for the lasting advantage of society has come to run the simultaneous and almost certain risk of judicial liability. The lesson is clear. Do not take the risk of making it better, simply make it more often.

Our unreasoning dependence upon the automobile as the primary source of essential economic wellbeing has deformed American cities to a point that actually endangers their future. Our excessive use of foreign and nonrenewable natural resources, such as petroleum, makes the continuation of current city design perilous. The shape of our cities, based almost entirely upon the irrational application of the ubiquitous family car, is not capable of simple change. We have allowed the automobile to alter personal relationships, deform daily activities, and endanger more balanced economic progress. The individual travel container has made us dependent upon both Saudi Arabia and Japan and there is little opportunity of escape. Our homes have become as diffuse as our government. Without gasoline we cannot even have neighbors.

The creative and destructive forces of our time are not easily measured. They are interrelated and actually require the perspective of distance for even a general understanding. The forces that we face as a society demand new and comprehensive visions. The problems cannot be solved by technicians alone. Where can we look for guidance?

As a nation, I believe that we must seek a comprehensive comparison of our values with those of the past. We should look at the independent citizens of smaller city states for the principles that guided such shapers of the world as those that built the temples at Karnak and the Greek Acropolis. What changes would the designers of such places suggest to us for use in our current condition? Would they give the same credance to the anonymous opinions that we so blandly accept every day? Would they give the same importance to proforma statements and abstract generalizations in lieu of demands for real proof? Would they support our current freedom to file false liability claims that make even the smallest construction variation a potential minefield of unpreventable financial losses? Would their interpretation of a reasonably judicious man be defined by the limber lips of our advertising agencies and unsavory plaintiffs' attorneys? I think not! I believe that these earlier innovators would carefully study our needs and cities as they now exist, and then undertake a more reasoned program of change.

It is indeed incredible that a really new and mechanically rational city has not been built in the twentieth century. The test, as I generally interpret the physical needs alone, involves a uniform method of accommodating varying functional sizes, coordinated transportation facilities, standardized utilities and services, and the control of three dimensional volumetric shapes rather than our ambiguous two-dimensional codal restraints. Services and utilities should be segregated and be made immediately accessible for connections, repair, and enlargement without the archaic practice of random burials and the perpetual digging-up of our streets. Several unified levels of vehicular and pedestrian access should be utilized and made uniform throughout most of our cities. Both new construction and demolition should be envisioned so that the entire city is an ever changing organism; however, consistent floor levels and supporting columns should be uniformly spaced. Apparently, such a system has not been built because of overlapping authorities. Multiple services and utilities continue to be buried in conflict with one another below a single vehicular surface that obviously serves too many masters. It is not the physical forces that present the problem. It is the conflicting and limited thinking of professionals such as public administrators, lawyers, accountants, engineers, architects, surveyors, and many other trades, that will not reconcile their selfish claims that make any reasonable coordination impossible.

It is patently obvious that any construction conceived by man cannot last forever. Each generation should recognize and build to satisfy new needs; however, it is wasteful to needlessly destroy human effort simply for lack of forethought or due to fallacious assumptions. As example, the misuse of the automobile cannot be continued. Widely accepted truths, no matter how highly esteemed, can still be absurd. The ultimate test must not always be limited to economic feasibility but should be measured by human use and happiness. Permanence, durability, and a sense of the eternal are important to man's psyche and the things that he gives his life to. Aimless change, often simply for the sake of financial gain, cannot be man's purpose on earth.

As we fly over our cities and look at their buildings we should appraise their qualities. Our cities should be highly personal and record their time in history. This is impossible if they are simply taken for granted and given no more thought than a passing cloud. The following three photographs illustrate strong and yet subtle contrasts, each to the others. Two are of the present-day cities of Hong Kong and Singapore and have been largely built during the last half century. The other, is of a religious precinct that is still in use after twenty-five centuries. The photographs have much to say about each other. Their underlying values are almost reciprocals of one another.

Photo 118, Hong Kong Harbor, from The Peak, 1983, overlooks much of Hong Kong, toward Kowloon. *Photo 119, Skyline and Boat Basin,*

Singapore, 1987, dramatizes the profile of many corporate masthead buildings. *Photo 120, Hypostyle Hall, Temple of Amun, Karnak, Egypt, 1980*, shows some of the 134 columns of the hall, each over forty feet in height and nine feet in diameter. These constructions, as recorded in time by photographs, contain messages to be interpreted by the viewer. Each, as a whole, encapsulates a cipher and represents its time, place, purpose, and people.

Hong Kong and Singapore represent an emerging "Asian Rim," the body of China and its immediate neighbors—The Orient. The mysterious East here meets the forces of our hallowed occident. Egypt with its occult faith, precedent to both Judaism and Christianity which overran Europe but not Asia, and the usual starting point of European history has its own well kept mysteries. In comparing these photographs we realize that the rabid division between East and West, Orient and Occident, is of recent origin and error. These people and their essential beliefs spring from many of the same roots and have the same sensibilities. It is largely time that separates them, time and intermediaries such as the Americas, for long before the Europeans overran North and South America they were settled by peoples originating in Asia, probably China.

Photo 118, Hong Kong Harbor, from the Peak, 1983, is a record of a British enclave located just off the coast of China since 1839, as seen from Victoria Peak on Hong Kong Island. The view overlooks the most energetic and productive areas of Kowloon and the New Territories. A dominant center for world commerce in the Far East, Hong Kong primarily consists of buildings of European heritage that house a largely oriental culture. A place of unparalleled vitality, it is undoubtedly the most beautiful harbor on earth. Whether looking inland toward the Chinese mainland or outward over the South China Sea there is a sense of power to the place, as seen from the Peak, that is unmatched. Other cities pale by comparison.

Even *Photo 119, Skyline and Boat Basin, Singapore, 1987*, does not have an equally dramatic site. As an independent republic since 1965 Singapore consists of small islands located off the south end of the Malay peninsula. The site is hilly rather than mountainous and is a very active, well located seaport and transshipment point. Like Hong Kong it was governed by the British between 1819 and 1963 and used as a naval stronghold.

The cultural traditions and governments of both cities are based upon English precedents but the dominant population is of Chinese origin. Both cities have enjoyed unbelievable growth since World War II, and while Singapore seems to expect stable growth along with most of Southeast Asia, Hong Kong will revert to China in 1997. Both cities are creatures of international treaties, trade, and geographic location. They are the physical results of creative mercantile and economic forces. Race, religion, and tradition seem to have had little effect upon their romantic

pasts as they reveled in the accomplishments of their own freebooters and human plunder.

The calm belief in the rectitude of time is seen in *Photo 120, Hypostyle Hall, Temple of Amun, Karnak, Egypt, 1980*. Here the faith of kings is inscribed by their priesthood in lasting hieroglyphic messages. A harbinger of cultures, governments, and religions to come, the stability of this African antiquity has never been duplicated. With human muscle alone these people built many of the greatest works of engineering in the history of the world. The very act of carving, transporting, and assembling these gigantic solid stone columns is simply beyond comprehension.

Are the people that built these miracles gone or has their system of beliefs and government merely changed? What brought about the seeming social deterioration or have they only developed different attitudes and aptitudes? What happened to their incentives, inventiveness, and leaders? Are cultures like flowers? Do they produce beautiful blossoms and then dry up and disappear? A continuing review of these three photographs of dissimilar but related social phenomena will allow the reader a better understanding of the forces that still guide us here on earth.

The modern towers of Hong Kong and Singapore create places for men to look outward toward the horizon, to new opportunities with a sense of collaborative power, while the temples at Karnak create mysterious, introverted, isolated, inner spaces where sun and darkness vie for psychic attention. One environment appears to be reclusive while the other overlooks the extrovert's exciting world.

The constructions of men exhibit their inner beliefs in many subtle and fragile ways, from columns with lotus blossoms as capitals to the location and grouping of corporate towers, but the genetic precedents are the same. We record our dreams and accomplishments variously but we all want to have them last and remembered.

The search for eternal, everlasting permanence appears to exist at our very core. Timeless and forever, every living person in one way or another, seeks sempiternal recognition. While we realize that it is only people who can recognize our accomplishments on this earth there are those who would forgo the opinion of contemporaries to achieve the extension of their accomplishments through time. This may have been the basis for many of the actions of the pharaohs.

Situated within the effervesence of three thousand five hundred years, how do you judge the progress of man? One of the world's most ancient and powerful cultures can here be compared to two of our most recently evolving city states. Has man used the intervening time well? Which of these cultural accomplishments will leave the most to our posterity? As with time itself, the only final reality lies within our own minds.

PART THREE: LIKING WHAT I SEE

I COMMUNICATION BETWEEN VIEW AND VIEWER

Liking what we see defines the ongoing process that we use in looking, really looking, at an object or view. Seeing represents decisions that must be sustained. As we look at something that we like, that attracts us, we ask ourselves, why? It is this self examination that allows us to look at even familiar objects in new ways.

As I look at an object or scene it is not a fixed and immutable image but an evolving communication composed of messages sent and messages received. I ask questions, answer them as best I can, then look and question again. Time after time these thought couriers go between my mind and my eye, between what the object looks like and what my brain tells me that I see, as I interpret this latest understanding of the object and balance these thoughts against what I already know. How many times must these messages be exchanged before enlarged reason and memory take hold?

Mystic though it may seem, looking is a type of two-way communication. As I look at objects and scenes, they speak to me in a series of messages of growing clarity. Seeing represents layers of thought and accumulated understanding. A favorite view from a study window embodies an evolving growth and appreciation that relates and contrasts such things as brilliant sunshine, gloomy storm clouds, twinkling lights, and leaves turning color in the fall. Nothing remains the same if we continue to seek the numen of the moment.

There is a mysterious quality to the act of looking. We know that we see only a fraction of what our eyes encompass. The thought has occurred to many before me, but I have a magical feeling that as I look, what I see is looking back at me. I feel that looking is more than satisfying an automatic appetite, more than mere consumption. Seeing is a joyous event for the one who looks and for what is seen. Both parties should relish the process of mutual appreciation.

In such a dream state, looking is not a precisely focused one-way street with messages only received. Dozens, even hundreds of round trip communications, may be recorded in our investigation of a single view or object. Exploring with the eye consists of communication from object, to eye, to brain and then back again, from brain, to eye, to object, over and over again. A ray of question, a returning light-beam of answer cycle back and forth in ever growing comprehension as we analyze what we see. Recognizing how, what, and why we see as we do involves this ever enlarging exchange between inanimate things and our very animate and inquiring eye-brain.

Physiologists tell us that our vision system takes up about half of our brain. They do not tell us how to effectively use this fifty percent of our mental capacity, and they often disclaim childhood mysteries and errant magic; however, coaching the mind accepts many mysteries and improbable associations. We have all knowingly deformed reality to stimulate desired reactions within ourselves. The methods used to achieve results need not always be founded in pure truth. Ask any psychiatrist or teacher!

Every academic discipline accepts its own distortions and develops its own special incantations. Each branch of learning recognizes "seeing" in a different way and since I am not able to understand many of their speculations I will continue to consider the process of seeing as if it occurred between two animate creatures.

The mechanism suggested here, where both the view and the viewer are attributed human intelligence, demands that we consider the continuous variability of both. Everything, all views and all viewers, are in perpetual change. For this reason our judgments must be made serially, but not by any right of absolute certainty. A tree, a lawn, a bird are many things and may be understood variously, but within every conception lies the inevitability of change. These layers of perception are held in place by a mystifying number of overlapping, interrelated, and associated categorical beliefs that have evolved slowly in each of us. They are continuously enlarged or diminished as we grow and age. We are routinely conditioned by what we see, whether considering a television audience or Pavlov's dogs, we must develop protective devices such as the boomerang questions that I propose asking inanimate things.

The assumption of two-way communication between the mind and what is seen justifies some unusual mental constructions. First, and of major importance, we must recognize that looking, seeing, is made up of a series of repeated acts that are separate in the beginning but are ultimately combined and integrated within the brain. The methodology is quite similar to that of parallel processing computers where the many parts of a problem are investigated simultaneously, and in a number of ways, quite unlike the conventional, centralized, one step at a time method of problem solving. Parallel processing, and the method of exchanging many, almost simultaneous messages between the mind and the object viewed accommodate a vast range of information and interpretations that is ultimately processed as a single resolution. The idea of the multiple inputs and a single final judgment can be visualized as though it consisted of thousands of local telephone exchanges, each compiling and editing a wide range of information that is finally sent to a central authority for harmonious adjudication.

II MATRIX FOR SELF EXAMINATION

We all have the capacity for at least three realms of seeing: conscious sight-thought, subconscious sight-feelings, and the creative synthesis of both. It is the reconciliation between conscious knowledge and subconscious feelings that brings forth our most significant understandings and creative acts.

It is possible to outline the essential differences between rational, conscious thought and romantic, subconscious feelings by a simple listing of their attributes. It is much more difficult to comprehend their origins and original causes, as outlined in *Appendix B*. It has been said that rational thought is only achieved through conscious effort while romantic insight comes mixed with our bones. This is simply not the case, for while heredity and our genetic composition certainly have great influence upon our intellects and our instincts they do not explain all real substance. The miracle of creative thought and true invention certainly combine genetic-heredity and learned-experience but something more contributes to the miracle.

The makeup of the individual brain is obviously linked to both inheritance and environment but the proportion of our total capacities used for reason and for feeling, apparently varies as widely as intellect itself. This may explain why so many of our most creative personalities have not possessed outstanding intellects. This is difficult to comprehend for intelligence quotients have come to represent the transcendent human attribute while creativity recedes into a mist of lesser significance. However, the fruits of the creative mind, rather than those of the memory limiting intellect, are the building blocks upon which the future will be built.

It is this belief that allows me the temerity to present a simplistic matrix for use in reconciling what we see in new ways. A picture or scene has many meanings. The procedure outlined here consists of a matrix upon which varying perceptions can be isolated and tested. A number of ultimate responses and reconciliations are possible. The measure of superiority lies solely within the mind of the observer. The viewer alone determines what is placed upon and what falls through the screening matrix.

The matrix proposed for isolating personally significant features of a visual image demands that the viewer distinguish between his interpretations of romantic insight and rational thought; developing symbols to isolate and define broad areas of potential perception and then allowing these forces to interact in an organized way.

The method briefly outlined in *Appendix B* can be used to comprehensively analyze the contents of a picture through the assumption that two-way visual exchange, between the viewer and the viewed object is possible. The interplay of rational thoughts and subconscious feelings are balanced as they eventually combine in the viewer's final synthesis.

The branch of philosophy known as ontology is concerned with the nature and relations of being and assumes that everything is of equal importance until proven otherwise. The relative importance of all that we see must receive our perpetual concern; the very nature of being must be continually tested. The crude matrix described in *Appendix B* includes the broad based scholarly disciplines and it is suggested that each photograph be tested within the parameters of such fixed criteria. When the strength of a belief is tested those aspects that resist change most severely define what we currently believe. Our lesser beliefs will fall under the spell of the moment and disappear. To determine what we really perceive as true, requires comparisons of relative strength. The force of our beliefs should be exposed to such widely ranging and established convictions, time after time, to test their validity. These assessments let us define the critical limits of our feelings and rational beliefs.

The strength of any belief, scientific or social, rests upon the outcome of broad-based tests that we construct for ourselves. Visual truth is subject to many measures, many disciplines, that are variously defined and polemically tested. Whether considering aspects of the general theory of relativity or current premises of the protective welfare state, validity may be recognized for the first time in some seemingly trivial scene.

A procedure that integrates interdisciplinary thinking allows us to probe our own minds for new understandings. Fitting our individual comprehensions into the grand plans of scholarly disciplines is both rewarding and frustrating. In some areas, as with the physical sciences, it is difficult to understand but simple to accept. In other disciplines, such as political science, it is simple to understand but difficult to accept. Yet the tenets of such disciplines can cross and may only be seen from a third, such as literature or the universal abstractions of mathematics. It is well to remember that no discipline is inviolable and all have skeletons somewhere within their closets.

The correlation of thoughs prompted by something seen, a photograph or an object, can be enlarged by passing it before the isolating forces of coordinated academic disciplines. These codified and packaged systems of knowledge represent the convictions of a group and have the added advantage of multiple defenders. It was so when the earth was held to be flat and it is equally true today. Truth must be supported by both pure reason and by allies. We cannot help recognizing this each evening as we watch the Six O'Clock News! A significant aspect of probing for visual insights must involve precise and objective order viewed simultaneously alongside our own personal and subjective preferences.

III   THE WISTFUL POINT OF VIEW

Having suggested a mechanical method for enlarging the act of seeing it is now essential to compromise all that I have said, for there are no formulas to control the mind-eye. Seeing and reason usually follow patterns accepted and systematized by the group, but change, real change, grows from idiosyncracies within the individual mind. So, in seeing

there is an indescribable probity that centers on the peculiar capacity and experience of the observer that cannot be duplicated. Each of us sees and feels the color of red, a distinct sunrise, or the unusual shape of a bell in a different way. A personal definition of such prosaic visual experiences enlarges our individuality for there are no replicas. Each of us holds a position founded in both likenesses and uniqueness from which we see and evaluate everything. From this grows a particular set of mental attitudes and opinions that can be called a *point of view*. It is this collection of individual beliefs and attitudes that separates each of us from society. Located at the very center of our being a point of view serves as the datum from which everything of value is measured. It is the balancing point of our own special identity. Our point of view is our most distinguishing characteristic and like the whorls on our finger tips it invariably separates us from others of our kind.

Everyone has a point of view even though it may seem practically indiscernible in the general population. Most people do not choose to take the time or effort to either recognize or to develop their essential differences. Society, particularly the great forces of the media, exerts enormous effort to eliminate individual differences and to cultivate a shapeless mass of compliant consumers. Identifying our own rudimentary character is the first step to personal awareness. Recognizing what we see and comprehend is a part of the process. This involves an inventory of *seeing what we like*.

At first our inventory of personal likes must be based upon attitudes and interpretations of the group, society, or our parents and associates who tell us what is good and bad. We arrive in this world much like a can of paint without color and seem to only have the capacity to accept color that may be added by others; however, at some point we should exert our own will.

Before such decisions can be made we must not only identify what we like but we should decide why, always realizing that visual convictions are like chameleons that constantly change their colors to match the surroundings. The relations between genes and environment are certainly not equivalent trains running on parallel tracks for they obviously have many switching points where they do interact. The same genes exposed to a childhood on the Texas prairie or a Harlem slum would evolve quite differently. Their responses to clouds, traffic, freedom, and the seasons would be very different. Aloneness, the innate reply to individual isolation, would be acceptable with the sweep of the prairie and rendered less tolerable to the crowded masses of New York's urban malaise. The same seeds, planted in different soils produce similar fruit but each results in some attributes becoming ascendant and superior to the others. It is these ascendant traits to which every individual must aspire as they analyze what they like and explore how their personal values came into being.

Taking inventory of the photographs shown here, a number of

psychological profiles are possible but such assessments were not sought. I have little use for the collective unconscious. The fallacy of self-centered animism is enough! All I seek is to understand why I like certain fleeting images more than others. From such determinations I may be able to alter my future beliefs and make clearer decisions.

Liking what we see demands the application of idiosyncratic questions that isolate a finite personal point of view, a way of looking, of asking questions of what you see that is special to you. The communication of these concepts and ideas between the viewer and the object gives direction to your psyche and enlarges your capacity for deeper self-examinations later.

Developing a better understanding of the sequence of our beliefs is very much like the processes underlying all design thought. As we look, the process moves from perceiving the whole before the parts, then analyzing the parts to better understand them, before again considering the whole. We establish a sequence of related parts and determinations, and then use comparisons and contrasts to project the known into the unknown. These individually preconceived mind-sets allow us to apply perceptions that are identified by seeing what we like. The sequence is always that of wanting, knowing, and then applying. There must be finite reasons for liking as we do and this defines our personal point of view.

Seeing what I like begins by accepting the mores of the group and is usually founded in an uninvestigated self and the acceptance of peer judgments. *Liking what I see* demands the identification of a special self. *Liking what I see* demands persistent exertion.

Creativity and humor have much in common with liking what we see, for as Madame de Sael said: "Wit consists of knowing the resemblance of things which differ, and the difference of things that are alike." I believe that original thought usually consists of recognizing the difference in things that are alike and the similarity of things that differ. It is the combining of non sequiturs, seeming and real, that initiate most original thought. The surprise of the "punch line" and the "idea" occur from the same unexpected realizations. The absurdity of an accepted use or the recognition of an unusual potential for change through design can startle and thereby create either humor or new conceptions. The ridiculous and the absurd can allow us to identify fresh relations and possibilities.

Original thought must begin within an individual mind, whether through new premises, recognitions, or logic and in whatever order they may occur. The detonating perception leading to a transforming idea usually lies between the two extremes of thought, one precise, rational, objective, conventional, codified, and accepted by the group and the other generalized, romantic, subjective, expansive, original, unorthodox, and in the beginning only acceptable to the individual. The underlying thought that allows such breaches of convention is almost always based upon new relationships. We are taught that sequiturs are the only proper subject for rational quests, but we eventually find that non sequiturs are the real trail blazers for emerging invention and casual thought. Fallacies can become as important as great truths when they serve as productive talismen. All conclusions need not flow from the same premises, for the premises themselves must often change. We owe a great debt to non sequiturs that allows us to recognize faltering premises that have become unduly sacred. These purging agents, whatever we may choose to call them, have no holy of holies. They are available to all of us. Non sequiturs are truly abstract in their function and they express qualities completely distinct from sacrosanct conventions. The dirty joke and the theory of thermodynamics have much in common.

As we look with our mind-eye it must be evident that so-called truth is of great importance but not so immutable that we develop a terror of being different, or even wrong. Real quality always involves the risk of grand mistakes. Truth itself changes.

Over a century ago Christian Doppler found that the lonely train whistle had a basis in fact. He observed that a train whistle going away from the listener was at a lower frequency than one approaching. Thirty years ago Edwin Hubble in a related recognition realized that distant galaxies were moving away from the solar system and inferred from this that the universe was expanding. From such innocuous recognitions powerful perceptions can grow. Confronted by these thoughts I suddenly realized that looking backward photographs taken years earlier are always somewhat different from my recollection of them. Invariably something not seen earlier is now evident. Layers of meaning have been added. My understanding has obviously changed, and while the image remains identical, the picture now in my mind-eye has almost invariably been altered in some way. Tracing these changing responses to their origins requires that I anticipate changes in other aspects of my experience. I not only recognize specific differences but have a better understanding of the comprehensive whole. New and idiosyncratic refinements have occurred. My personal interpretation of minor, everyday objects and scenes is not the same today as when the photograph was originally taken. Have I changed? Has the photograph been a part of altering my perception of life, my point of view? The answer to both questions is *yes*!

To live and to see fully, completely, perfectly, presumes clairvoyance and a heaven here on earth. Such aims are unattainable, so how do we decide upon our worldly objectives? How do we find a point of view that is both realizable and worthwhile? If we are to live and see as fully as possible we must believe that we have peculiar capacities that will let us creatively participate in the evolution of our kind. In so doing we will reject the enigmatic and inscrutable and look in purposeful new ways.

The desire to recognize original truths should infuse all of our efforts. This wistful point of view, with its vague yearnings and growing demands will let us know when we are near a new beginning. When the eerie image appears we will recognize what we see.

APPENDIX A

Twenty thousand fleeting glances of very different visual moments had to be reduced to 120 colored slides. Economics demanded the elimination of over 166 slides for each one retained and during the intervening fourteen years the condition of the events and the recorder of the events had both changed.

The selection process required a year of intermittent viewing and agonizing. The procedure can be summarized as having had five stages, including: 1) the ad hoc, subjective, personal selection of an initial 248 slides; 2) the division of these slides into twenty loosely defined categories of assumed characteristics; 3) the placing of each slide into one of these subgroups through a process of weighing and grading that reduced the number to 141; 4) the further refining of the categories of characteristics and the reduction of the slides to the ultimate 120; and 5) the final combining of subject matter categories to the fourteen shown in the Table of Contents.

The rules for selection were often and autocratically changed and expanded while the number of categories was consistently simplified and reduced. Looking backward upon the labored process and the resulting evolution of my own thoughts, I question the value of this massive effort to quantify the qualitative. The consistency of my own judgment does not seem to have improved. My inability to interpret quality, in the part, makes the measure of the whole seem irrelevant and suspect. The process can be used to trace where I have been but it is apparently useless in guiding me to where I would like to go. The effort may have made me see with greater sensitivity but certainly not with greater assurance.

APPENDIX B

It is clear to me that my subconscious feelings could have as much influence upon my visual judgments as conscious knowledge. Our visual decisions continuously pit RATIONAL THOUGHT and ROMANTIC INSIGHT. We know that both forces are essential and intimately related; however, RATIONAL THOUGHT soon dissipates itself unless another ROMANTIC INSIGHT shows it the way to the future. A fuller comprehension of this thought can be illustrated by the following comparisons:

RATIONAL THOUGHT	ROMANTIC INSIGHT
CONSCIOUS KNOWLEDGE Beliefs and Precepts Objective, Pragmatic Logic	SUBCONSCIOUS FEELINGS Intuitions and Presentations Subjective Preferences
INVOLVES REASON AND PROCESS Intellectual—Reasonable Experience, Memory, Knowledge	INVOLVES HABITS AND EXTERNAL PERCEPTION Instinctual—Emotional Feelings, Potential Causes, Original Premises
COGNITIVE AND VOLITIONAL Ultimately Lucid Known Phenomena	CONATIVE AND SPONTANEOUS Profound Sensibility Clairvoyant
SEEKS UNDERLYING LOGIC AND REASON A Logic That Is Inescapable Seeks Universal Truth	SEEKS A NEW SENSUAL UNDERSTANDING Conditioned To See New Possibilities Seeks New Insights
FULLNESS OF MEANING Facts—Reason Do It Best	ALTERED HUMAN RESPONSE Feelings—Beliefs Do It First
CONSCIOUS EXPLANATION Highest Efficiency Measure	SUBCONSCIOUS ORIGIN Purest Innovation Potential
VISUAL REALITY	VISUAL POTENTIALITY

Such a comparison can be arranged as Cartesian coordinates with RATIONAL THOUGHT spread across the horizontal, or X-X axis, and ROMANTIC INSIGHT listed down the Y-Y axis. Four major categories, or subdivisions, can be listed on both axes. Reading horizontally, under RATIONAL THOUGHT, I propose four vertical columns of: Nature & Natural, Humanities, Sciences, and Conscious Origins. Reading downward, under ROMANTIC INSIGHT, the four lines I propose are: Feelings, Beginnings, Deviations, and Subconscious Origins.

Further subdivision of these headings, under RATIONAL THOUGHT, allows Humanities to become History & Philosophy, Art & Literature, and Universal Abstractions. Under Sciences we find: Physical, Biological, and Social-Behavioral. A similar detailing of ROMANTIC INSIGHT shows Feelings broken into Emotion, Instinct, and Sensation; Beginnings divided into Culture, Mythology, and Tradition; and Deviations separated into Morality, Mystery, and Superstition.

These subdivisions allow eight vertical columns of RATIONAL THOUGHT on the horizontal X-X axis and ten lines of ROMANTIC INSIGHT on the vertical Y-Y axis. The intersection of columns and lines produce touchstones for comparison and provides an organized method of considering the forces acting between these apparent extremes. There are eighty possible confluences and contacts in the diagram described.

Using this diagramatic matrix to relate intersecting possibilities it must be noted that RATIONAL THOUGHT should always begin with Nature & Natural and extend through Conscious Origins. ROMANTIC INSIGHT should begin with Feelings and extend beyond Subconscious Origins. In this search for new truths the intersections between columns and lines provide fresh wayposts for individual comparison and thought. A reconciliation between Conscious and Subconscious Origins must eventually be made.

Such diagrams with their broad categories of concern can be adapted to the needs of the scene and the individual attempting to understand the vast range of possibilities lying between RATIONAL THOUGHT and ROMANTIC INSIGHT. The need for exact definitions in such mental constructions is outweighed by the opportunities for personal comprehension and use.

There are strong institutional forces acting through the eight vertical columns and the ten horizontal lines represented by these word symbols. As these lines of perception intersect and interact the sieve of our artificially induced reason catches and reinforces our more pertinent findings. The others fall through the cracks of our memory. With time and use, and without visualizing the precise geometric relationships, the interrelated forces diagrammed here can be applied in instantaneous, repeated, and almost stroboscopic visual analyses that we make of what we see. The habit of always relating Conscious Knowledge and Subconscious Feelings is central to all of our visual judgments.

ONE HUNDRED TWENTY PHOTOGRAPHS

1

5

7

9

11

13

15

19

21

25

29

31

35

39

41

43

45

49

53

57

59

61

67

69

73

75

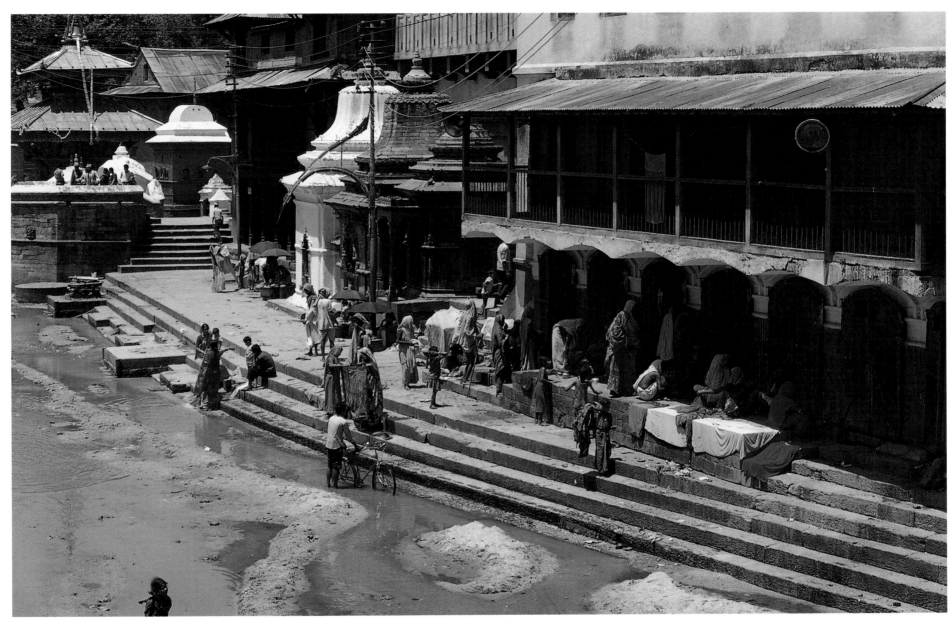

81

83

91

93

95

97

99

103

107

113

115